Treasure Trails of the Southwest

Treasure Trails of the Southwest

Marc Simmons

University of New Mexico Press
Albuquerque

For
My Trail Friends
the Galloways,
Jim, Nancy, Erin, and Marc

Library of Congress Cataloging-in-Publication Data
Simmons, Marc.
  Treasure trails of the Southwest / Marc Simmons. — 1st ed.
    p. cm.
Includes bibliographical references.
  ISBN 0–8263–1510–0. — ISBN 0–8263–1509–7 (pbk.)
  1. Treasure-trove—Southwest, New. 2. Southwest, New–History,
Local. I. Title.
F799.S63 1994   *93–42191*
979—dc20   *CIP*

Contents

Preface   *vii*
1   *The Golden Statue*   3
2   *El Chato's Treasure*   11
3   *The Hill of Gold*   18
4   *The Gold Nugget*   23
5   *The Meaning of Gran Quivira*   28
6   *Indian Treasure*   32
7   *Turquoise Has Played a Part*   36
8   *Quest for the Blue Mountains*   41
9   *Manzano's Mysterious Stranger*   47
10   *Twists of Circumstance*   51
11   *A Silver Cache*   57

CONTENTS

12   The Tucson Meteorite Anvil   61

13   Did Ancient Europeans Wander the Southwest?   66

14   La Mina del Padre   70

15   In the Shadow of the San Mateos   75

16   The Lost Gold of San Rafael   81

17   Train Robber's Loot   87

18   The Adams Diggings   92

19   Salt on the Frontier   98

20   From a Prospector's Notebook   103

21   The Ghosts of Kingston   107

22   New Mexico's Placers   112

23   Treasures of the Pinos Altos   117

24   Boom Days in Mogollon   121

25   The German's Knapsack   125

26   Lost Gold, Found?   132

27   Spanish Gold or Fraud?   139

APPENDIX ONE: A WPA TALE SAMPLER

Treasure of the Plum, José Trujillo   146

The Padre's Mine at Cañon de la Soledad,
Cleofas M. Jaramillo   146

Buried Money on the Mimbres River,
Frances E. Totty   148

Treasure, Ramitos Montoya   150

APPENDIX TWO: TREASURE ITEMS FROM THE NEWSPAPERS

A Note on the Adams Diggings   152

A Hint to Prospectors   152

A Bizarre Hoax   154

Lost Spanish Mine Found   160

Selected References   162

Preface

I heard my first lost-mine yarn when I was just a youngster. The teller was an old man who ran a small shop on
a side street near the Santa Fe plaza. When he saw that I
was enthralled by everything related to the desert Southwest, he shared his story.

As a young man, he had gone with a friend to do some
prospecting in the dry and isolated mountain ranges of
Baja California. With a string of burros carrying supplies
and equipment, they traveled far into the back country.

Finally, their searches turned up some promising looking ore. But then my narrator's companion fell from a
ledge fracturing his leg and collar bone. Since he was
unable to travel, his friend made him as comfortable as
possible. Taking three of the burros, he started for help.

Two days later, the shopkeeper said to me, he was out
of water and lost. He felt panic setting in when suddenly

the burros raised their heads, twitched their ears, and started forward at a fast clip. They had smelled water.

"Soon we came to a dark, foul smelling pool," he continued. "Two of the burros thrust their noses in and began to drink heavily. But the third stepped back and refused to have anything to do with the stuff. I was so thirty I drank a couple of handfuls, but gagged and had to stop.

"Almost immediately I fell sick and lay doubled up for several hours. By then the two burros that had quenched their thirst were dead. Taking hold of the tail of the remaining animal for support, I set out again. Eventually some mountain people found me, almost dead, and days later I awoke in a hospital. A search party was sent to look for my friend but he was never found."

Ending his tale, the old man said to me that the incident had killed forever his interest in prospecting. And he added, "You know, if that third burro hadn't been smart enough to avoid the poison water, you wouldn't be listening to this story now."

What he told me awakened my interest, not in searching for lost mines and buried treasure, but in hearing or reading the accounts of people who had. Not long afterward, I stumbled upon a copy of J. Frank Dobie's book, *Coronado's Children.* It was probably the earliest popular work to describe the searches for some of the Southwest's most elusive treasures.

Coronado, way back in 1540, had been the first to enter the region hoping to strike it rich. But he failed, as did most of the horde of slightly mad adventurers who came after him. Some of them tore up the land, drained lakes, and even changed the courses of rivers in a frenzied scramble for quick wealth. Many lost their lives.

Dobie, who interviewed a large number of latter-day treasure-seekers, found that the real riches lay in the stories surrounding their years of questing for the pot of gold at the end of the rainbow. Fascinated, I read his accounts of such famous lodes and treasures as the Lost San Saba Mine, Maximillian's Gold, and the Breyfogle Mine.

When I went to Austin to enter the University of Texas as an undergraduate, I made a point of visiting Dobie, who lived only a few blocks from the campus. Gradually, I steered the conversation around to lost mines, and he told me how he had managed to collect some of the information that went into *Coronado's Children*.

I had my copy along, so I asked him to inscribe something in the front. This is what he wrote: "I guess there is no lesson in this book, but you might deduce (in Robert Louis Stevenson's phrase) that 'it's better to travel hopeful than to arrive.' "

That sums up a good deal about the treasure-hunting phenomenon. Those who become a part of it, of course, are hoping to become instant millionaires. But if they keep looking for years, the search itself soon becomes an obsession and a way of life.

A good example in recent times was the late Doc Milton Noss, who first brought to public notice Padre LaRue's treasure, supposedly hidden on Victorio Peak inside New Mexico's White Sands Missile Range. Noss claimed he stumbled upon this horde of Spanish gold in a cave, while deer hunting, and brought out eighty-eight bars. When he tried to enlarge the cave entrance with dynamite, it collapsed and he could never get back inside.

A similar feature occurs in many lost treasure stories: someone makes a discovery, then loses the location, and spends the remainder of his life looking for it. Other cases involve a treasure map, often spirited out of a monastery in Mexico, whose directions to buried riches are too vague to pinpoint, except in a general way, the actual site of the bonanza.

And then there are some yarns, containing directions, that are simply passed along by word of mouth. In my own town of Cerrillos, New Mexico, I've long heard how Black Jack Ketchum once held up the express car on the Santa Fe Railroad. He is said to have buried (and never recovered) the loot near a large rock formation three miles east of town.

Trouble with this is I can find no record of Black Jack ever holding up trains hereabouts. But then, maybe I haven't dug deeply enough into old newspapers and legal records.

I have a friend who works in the archives in Santa Fe. He tells me that once a shabbily dressed elderly man came in and demanded to be shown all the old treasure maps kept on file.

When told that no such maps were available, he expressed both disbelief and anger. "Well, if you don't have them, you should!" he said. "Then poor folks like me could go out and find a treasure, and not be poor anymore."

His complaint brings to mind a statement made by the great American author Washington Irving in *Tales of the Alhambra,* his engaging book on Spain. Therein can be found this insightful passage: "I have remarked that the stories of treasure buried by the Moors which prevail throughout Spain are most current among the poorest

A prospector's equipment. Courtesy Marc Simmons Collection.

people. It is thus kind nature consoles with shadows for want of substantials."

Treasure stories, he is saying, tend to flourish among those most in need of hope. The lottery in our own day perhaps fills something of the same need. But understanding this phenomenon helps to explain why Hispanic folklore of the Southwest is so rich in this type of tale. Anglo Americans, upon entering the country in the nineteenth century, listened to the yarns as they were spun around campfires between the Pecos and the Rio Colorado, and many were led to launch their own searches, in the simple expectation that something of value really did lay hidden and that it could be found, with luck and dedicated effort.

Another noted literary figure, Joseph Conrad, made his own observation on such matters. "There is no getting away from a treasure that once fastens upon your mind," he wrote. "A man will curse the day he ever heard of it, but he will never forget it until he is dead." In his words can be found confirmation of the powerful allure exerted by treasure tales.

For years I have been writing short articles on hidden treasures and lost mines, and my fascination with the subject has continued to grow. It seemed time to gather together some of my favorite pieces and offer them as a collection to those readers with a special interest in southwestern lore. Some of the oldest stories may sound familiar, even though I have worked them over with the aim of imparting a new freshness. In other cases, I have dug into obscure records, permitting me to recount a tale that is largely unknown.

In sum, the configuration of this book was shaped by the folk traditions still alive and well in the American

Southwest. I extend an invitation, therefore, to load up your burro with pick, shovel, gold pan, and canteen and set forth with me on wispy trails in pursuit of adventure and fortune. You will not be disappointed!

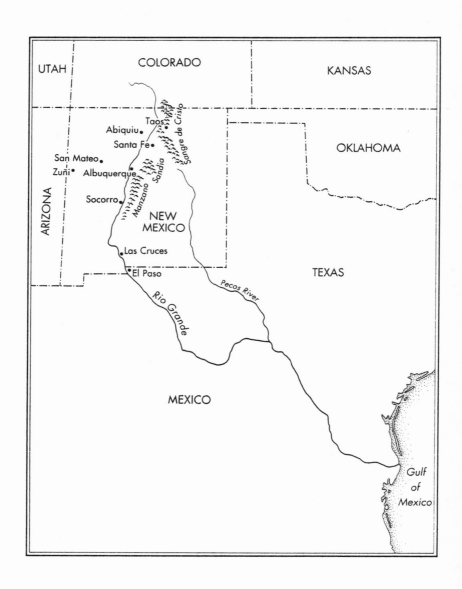

"The stories of golden mountains, of buried millions, and of mysterious lost mines in New Mexico alone would fill a volume."

—CHARLES F. LUMMIS, 1912

1
The Golden Statue

The story of the golden statue has its genesis in the expedition of the Franciscan friar Francisco Silvestre Vélez de Escalante. In the summer of 1776, he set forth with eight companions in an attempt to open a trail from New Mexico across the Great Basin to California.

Leaving Santa Fe, the little party pushed up the Chama Valley and, by the first week of August, reached the vicinity of the modern Durango, Colorado. After examining the surrounding mountains, the men headed northwest across Utah. By the end of September, heavy snows had fallen in the mountain passes and blocked the way west. So a decision was made to abandon the expedition and, following a swing south into Arizona, the little cavalcade arrived back in Santa Fe on the day after New Year's Day of 1777.

On balance, the strenuous project had been a failure, for New Mexico remained unlinked by road to California.

Nevertheless, much had been accomplished in the way of exploration, since in the course of 159 days of travel the Escalante expedition had covered a good seventeen hundred miles, most of it passing through country unfamiliar to the Spaniards. And there was one other result of interest. In his reports, Father Escalante spoke of finding promising mineral signs in what is now southwestern Colorado.

That information surely stirred the blood of some of colonial New Mexico's more enterprising citizens. For long, fortune seekers had been prowling the high country bracketing the upper Rio Grande Valley, and, we have every reason to believe, making an occasional strike. Documentary evidence of this, however, is almost nonexistent, for the mining was usually carried on illegally and in secret.

The Spanish king claimed ownership of all mineral rights in the empire. To encourage mining development, he allowed individuals to stake claims and extract ore, when they found it. But the king took his share of the production. His cut was the royal *quinto*, a one-fifth tax of all precious metals recovered.

In our isolated Southwest, Spanish prospectors who stumbled upon a gold or silver lode were apt to keep silent about it. They could carry on quietly small-scale mining, crush and smelt the ore, and smuggle the crude bars out of the area, without paying the *quinto.*

Evidence of such activity is found in the Spanish *arrastres* or primitive ore crushers. Remnants of these simple devices occur in remote locations from the Colorado Rockies southward to the vicinity of El Paso. *Arrastres* operated by burro power. A central post was sunk in the ground and a movable beam attached to it. The far end of the beam was hitched to a donkey who was driven in a circle around the post.

4

Mexican *arrastre* or ore crusher. A mule or donkey at the end of the rope turns the heavy stones. Courtesy Arizona Historical Society, neg. no. 408.

Flagstones, placed in the ground, formed a circular floor. Over this, granite boulders tied to the beam by ropes were dragged, crushing ore in a mortar and pestle effect. Today, around traces of these old *arrastres*, pieces of black slag often can be picked up. They are evidence that a crude furnace for smelting also once existed on the site.

The residents of northern New Mexico must have heard, by word of mouth, that Father Escalante had chanced upon some alluring mineral signs during his wanderings.

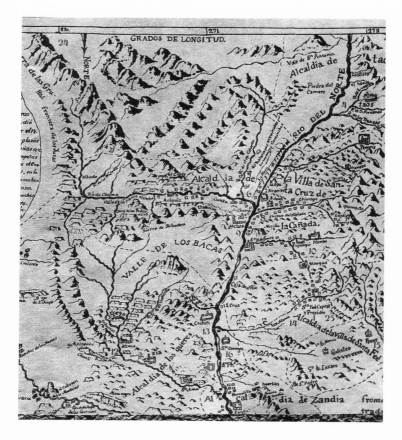

Spanish map of the 1770s showing Colorado mountains at upper left, location of the Josephine Mine and cave of the Golden Statue. Courtesy Marc Simmons Collection.

Their location, unfortunately, was far outside the familiar range of travel, and even more disturbing, it lay within the country of the mountain-dwelling Utes, a tribe then at war with the New Mexicans.

Those circumstances perhaps explain why no one immediately rushed to follow up on the Escalante reports. Yet they were not forgotten, and as time drifted by, with the northwestern frontier remaining quiet, men all along the Rio Grande began to cast wistful glances in that direction. Finally, a company of miners banded together, and well armed and supplied, they rode up the Chama Valley, passed the outpost village of Abiquiu, and crossed the Continental Divide.

Ascending to the high country of Colorado, within the region now called the Four Corners, they went to prospecting. Shortly, the search was vindicated, for the party struck a vein of gold and began tunneling into a mountainside. The ore was rich beyond their wildest imaginings, and visions of a bright future, brimming with wealth, must have filled every head.

Members of the company decided to name their find the *Mina de Josepha,* or the Josephine Mine. Likely, it was in honor of the wife or sweetheart of one of their number. Carefully, they built *arrastres* and a furnace to handle the gold ore, and their small ingots grew in a pile. Then as the cold winds began to slide off the shoulders of the Rockies, foretelling the approach of winter, the toiling miners determined they had reaped enough, at least for that season. They would seal the mine entrance and start for home. But before the return could be undertaken, they fell to quarreling over how their treasure ought to be divided.

Before matters came to blows, one of the men offered a solution. They would melt down the gold and, forming a mold in the sand, would cast a statue of the Christ Child. The image could be easily transported to Santa Fe, and once there the parish priest might be consulted as to the proper disposition of the gold. That pious suggestion appealed to the entire company, and so it was done.

Loading up their newly cast golden statue, the New Mexicans turned homeward. But just a few miles down the trail, they fell into an ambush laid by their foes, the Utes. The men forted up inside some boulders and fought valiantly. It soon became clear, however, that the situation was hopeless. The defenders, therefore, held a huddled council. They agreed to draw lots, and the two miners thus chosen were to slip through the Indian lines at night with the holy statue. The others, staying behind, pledged to hold off the Utes as long as possible. The statue bearers did manage to escape, and their abandoned companions, we presume, were subsequently massacred. At least, so far as the records show, nothing was ever heard of them again.

For two days the pair of survivors struggled through rough country, avoiding the main trail for fear of the Indians. Then, becoming exhausted from carrying the weighty statue, they elected to hide it in a cave. It was placed on a rock ledge, just inside the opening. As best they could, the men drew a simple map of the cave's location, and after that, they hurried on with their flight, eventually reaching Santa Fe. Accounts say that both miners were so frightened of the Utes that they were never willing to return and recover what they had concealed. Others, it is claimed, who followed copies of their map attempted to locate the cave with its precious statue and to find the Josephine Mine, but without success.

The story lived on and in 1901 was learned by a young prospector from California named Al Hainey. He showed up in northern New Mexico, asked a few questions, and was directed to a fellow named Francisco Olguin. It seemed that Olguin was a direct descendant of one of the miners who had escaped with the golden statue, and he owned the original map. Hainey persuaded him that they should join forces and conduct a search. The two set out for the lower corner of Colorado and, based on the map, began to explore the La Plata Mountains. At one point, they discovered an arrow marker scratched in a volcanic rock, a symbol once commonly used to indicate treasure. It pointed toward a cave which proved to be empty, but it was not clear whether they had found the right cave, the one visited by Olguin's ancestor.

A few days later, the pair came upon the remains of an *arrastre* and scattered chunks of metallic slag. Clearly, Spanish miners had once worked here. For more than a week, Hainey and Olguin scoured the surrounding mountainsides, hoping to find the concealed mouth of the Josephine Mine. No luck!

On one slope, Al Hainey picked up some gleaming chunks of stone that felt heavy in his palm. Olguin pronounced them fool's gold, so he thrust a couple of samples in his pocket and forgot about them. Soon the men gave up looking and parted company, Francisco Olguin taking a sheepherder's job and Al Hainey going back to California, still carrying pieces of his fool's gold as a souvenir.

Thirty years later, Hainey happened to run across his souvenirs in a box. Out of curiosity, he took them to an assay office to be tested. The specimens proved to be ore, containing fifty thousand dollars worth of gold per ton. Returning to the La Plata Mountains, he was unable to pinpoint the spot where he and Olguin, three decades earlier, had seen the *arrastre* and had picked up the lumps of "fool's gold."

To this day, there are people who continue to believe that the statue of gold still rests secure in its natural vault, just where the Spanish miners first left it. They believe as well that the Josephine Mine remains hidden, quietly waiting to be rediscovered. And, of course, there is a slim possibility that they might be right.

2

El Chato's Treasure

It seems to me there are two kinds of people who pursue buried-treasure stories: first, those who hope to find a treasure and get rich; and second, persons who are interested in the yarns themselves, as collectible folklore. I fall in the second category. Treasure tales, I've found, are seldom based on solid history. The details have often been handed down by word of mouth, becoming hopelessly jumbled in the process. But even in the most garbled story, it is sometimes possible to find a few crumbs of truth.

Such is the case in the tale of El Chato's treasure. What I relate here is actually the distillation of several different versions, boiled down to produce some semblance of a plausible account. It begins with a renegade and highwayman of Spanish colonial days, Pedro Narvaez, or Nevarez, who went by the nickname El Chato, meaning Pug Nose.

In a brush with royal soldiers, a sword had cut off the end of his nose.

El Chato headed a band of cutthroats whose hideout lay in the Organ Mountains. For a decade, they attacked stray travelers, pack trains, and wagon caravans passing through the Mesilla Valley of southern New Mexico. El Chato's most spectacular raid occurred near the end of his bloody career. The target was a party of missionary friars from Mexico City. Their pack mules were loaded with silver coin and with gold vessels for the churches of Santa Fe.

The bandits swooped down on the train and with loud yells ran off the mules, loads and all. The dismayed friars could do nothing but walk back to El Paso, the nearest settlement, and report the crime. El Paso's military commander sent south for reinforcements. He also enlisted citizen volunteers who had their own grudges to settle with the bandits.

When all was ready, the force marched up the Rio Grande. The soldiers were dressed as merchants and kept their weapons hidden. Their disguises worked. El Chato, seeing rich pigeons ready for plucking, fell into the trap. In a furious battle, all the attackers were either killed or captured. One of the prisoners was El Chato. Marched off to Mexico City under guard, he was tried for his crimes, condemned to death, and hanged.

But what of the mule loads of treasure stolen from the missionaries by the outlaw gang? Did any of them divulge its whereabouts while they were in Spanish hands? The answer with regard to El Chato is confusing. Some accounts say he went to the gallows with lips sealed. But others claim that he revealed the treasure location to the priest who gave him last rites.

In any case, written directions to the treasure have been handed down, and many fortune hunters have tried to follow them. El Chato's hoard is supposedly buried in two connecting caves with a single sealed entrance, which faces three conical peaks. Some residents of Las Cruces used to go about the Organ Mountains setting off small charges of dynamite. They hoped the explosions would echo underground and disclose any cave, or perhaps start a landslide and open the entrance.

In 1934, the noted folklorist Dr. Arthur L. Campa was hunting deer in the Magdalena Mountains west of Socorro. By chance, he met and became friends with another hunter, Ben Brown. In conversation around the campfire, Brown casually remarked that he had discovered the location of El Chato's cave. "It's not in the Organs, like everyone has thought," he said, "but in the next range to the north. I found it by accident one day, and ever since I go back in my spare time and dig away. Over the centuries the tunnel has filled in with loose dirt."

Campa was interested, so Ben Brown offered to show him the site. They drove down, and sure enough there was a cave entrance under three conical peaks.

"For a short distance we walked upright," Campa explained later. "Then we crawled on all fours til the cave split into a Y. I went one way and Ben the other." Finally, Dr. Campa was forced to crawl on his stomach, and then suddenly he became stuck in the narrow tunnel. He remained wedged for an hour, and panic seized him. But at last, he felt Brown pulling on his ankles and he was quickly jerked free.

Outside again, he thankfully took in the daylight and fresh air. Ben Brown displayed a colonial mining tool and a Spanish coin that had been uncovered earlier. "Yes sir,

Organ Mountains, burying place of El Chato's treasure, according to some of the early legends. Courtesy Museum of New Mexico, neg. no. 106905.

there's treasure down there," he proclaimed. But after his unnerving experience, Dr. Campa decided he wanted no more of that cave. He kept up with his friend over the years, but so far as he learned, Ben Brown never did bring up El Chato's treasure.

I published this story several years ago, and, in response, received a letter from El Paso businessman Charles H. Leavell. He provided me with some new information, including the directions to the treasure cache that Pedro Navarez is supposed to have left. This data placed the location at an entirely different site.

"In 1898," Mr. Leavell began, "my father owned a large ranch at Clint, Texas. His widowed sister, Kate Leavell Sharp, had befriended the local padre of nearby San Lorenzo Mission. When the priest died, he left her a crude map and the document describing the whereabouts of El Chato's cave. She later gave both items to her school, the University of Texas, but not before my uncle, John H. Leavell, had made a copy of them."

Charles Leavell sent me the directions, saying, "You'll note that this document places the treasure in the mountains of Mexico, just southeast of Ciudad Juárez, and not in the Organ Mountains as you reported." Studying the paper he had sent, I found that was indeed the case. "In 1901 my father and my uncle, who was ten years younger and just out of MIT, decided to conduct a search. They organized a group of treasure seekers and rode across the Rio Grande on horseback. In their packs were dynamite, picks, and shovels. Within two days they discovered the cave.

"The setting was exactly as described in the document. But it was clear that the cave had been entered

15

already by someone and no treasure could be found. My Dad did find old sandals, cooking utensils, and a simple cross made of cottonwood. He was nervous about being there and so retreated back to his ranch with no loot. He recounted the adventure on many occasions to friends and family."

In his youth that tale made a strong impression on Charles Leavell, and he informed me that in 1958 he decided to try to revisit the cave explored more than a half-century earlier by his father. In the planning, he enlisted El Paso artist and writer Tom Lea as well as his uncle, John Leavell, now an old man, who came out from Tulsa. They drove to Finley, Texas, and picked up an aging rancher, Jess Walbridge. He too had been part of the original expedition. Then they drove to the banks of the Rio Grande.

The two old-timers pointed out the distant round hill and peaks described in the document and which marked the site of the treasure cave. They also instructed the younger men to be sure and look up Juan Sanchez in the Mexican village of El Porvenir. He would know about the treasure. Mr. Leavell told me that later he did contact Sanchez and made arrangements for saddle horses and pack burros to transport himself and seven companions. Tom Lea had become ill and was unable to go.

It was a hard ride through rough country, he related. "The cave was perched on a ledge about 100 feet from the valley floor. Three of our party roped up, then hauled me up. Everything was just as the document pictured it. The cave had been partially closed with caliche, cemented with burro blood. Back in the floor at the center of the cave was a deep depression, as if something had been removed. In another cave to the left was a sturdy wooden cross and evidence of human occupation."

The Leavell party had brought along a metal detector, and it too was carried up by rope. "Deep in the cave, it began to ping," he explained. "We frantically dug and to my utmost chagrin we uncovered a Pet Milk can." In closing his letter to me, Charles Leavell declared: "That is my story and I am sorry my cave is far from the one you wrote about north of the Organ Mountains in New Mexico." And he added, "The villagers of El Porvenir still refer to El Chato as a hero, almost a legendary Robin Hood. Their folklore is fascinating to hear."

Other versions of El Chato's treasure cave may well surface someday. The mysteries surrounding such stories defy all attempts to put them to rest.

3
The Hill of Gold

The epic of fortune hunting in the colonial Southwest has provided us with a trove of familiar
stories that over the years have made their way into
the pages of printed books. Yet at least one early-day
treasure hunt of the Spaniards has passed almost
unnoticed. It concerns a quest, late in the Spanish
period, for a rumored Cerro de Oro, or Hill of Gold.
The few details left to us are found scattered through
the yellowing, mouse-chewed documents in the old
colonial archives at Santa Fe.

The chief actor in this tale was a disabled soldier named
Bernardo de Castro—a perfect model of "the little man"
who led a fascinating life, but whose exploits never found
their way into the history books. In the mid-1790s, Bernardo, with the rank of sergeant, was fighting Indians
around Chihuahua City. In one skirmish he suffered a

severe lance wound in the leg, a misfortune that forced him to retire and accept a government pension.

Being of a restless nature, Bernardo decided that as soon as he could hobble about, he would go to New Mexico and start a new career. In Santa Fe, sometime early in 1798, he got together a large herd of cattle and several wagons filled with merchandise and set out for El Paso. Along the way Apaches struck, running off all the stock, burning the wagons, and killing a number of the drivers. Bernardo de Castro barely escaped with his life.

Back in Santa Fe, he borrowed money for a new stake and went to trading with the roving Comanches on the eastern plains. Returning from one of his trips, he found the capital all agog. A few days before, a Frenchman had suddenly appeared from the east, asking to speak with the governor, Don Fernando Chacón. Ushered into the old adobe palace, the stranger had displayed a lump of sparkling metal. It had come, he said, from a place well known to the Indians—a hill of solid gold, lying eight or nine days journey across the plains. If the governor would give him an escort of soldiers, he would go and show the Spaniards this Cerro de Oro.

Chacón acted quickly. He assembled a squad of mounted troops and sent them hurrying off with the beguiling Frenchman. The gold seekers had been gone three days when Bernardo de Castro reached Santa Fe and first heard the story. Going directly to the governor, he asked and received permission to pursue the expedition and join it.

By fast riding, he caught up with the party as it was entering the broad expanse of the Llano Estacado, the Staked Plains. Later, the sly Frenchman sneaked away from camp and disappeared. The Spaniards had been tricked! The leaders now gave up in discouragement and turned back toward Santa Fe. But not Bernardo de Castro. He had been bitten by the gold bug, and alone he decided to continue the search.

Days later, he wandered into a Comanche village where earlier he had done some trading. When he told his story, the Indians laughed. They knew that Frenchman. He had come to them with some trinkets to swap and they had sold him the chunk of gold. There was a Hill of Gold, sure enough, but that stranger didn't know where it was. The Comanches knew, though, and they offered to take their

The Round Mountain in northeastern New Mexico, near the Colorado border, where Sergeant Bernardo de Castro searched for the Hill of Gold. Courtesy Marc Simmons Collection.

friend Don Bernardo there so that he could fill his pockets with the glittering metal.

Poor Bernardo de Castro. The end of the rainbow was in sight, but his horse was worn out with hard traveling and he had no pack mules. He wanted to load mules, not pockets, with gold. So he decided to return to Santa Fe and enlist the governor's help for a full-scale expedition. His guides, he hoped, would wait for him.

Back in the capital, he got a rude shock. Governor Chacón, with the failure of the first search, had lost interest. He not only refused aid, he denied Bernardo permission to return to the plains. The old soldier now settled upon a daring plan. He would journey to Mexico City and seek an interview with the Viceroy. If he could convince that high official of the existence of the Cerro de Oro, then all obstacles for another expedition would be removed.

Bernardo started southward on his decrepit horse. But, in the desert above El Paso, the tired creature collapsed and died. Since there was nothing else to be done, the man began walking, on his game leg, toward Mexico City almost two thousand miles away. Months later he arrived ragged, scarecrow-thin, and penniless. In that condition there seemed little chance that he could gain an interview with the Viceroy. For days Bernardo de Castro wandered through the streets of the city, begging alms and telling anyone who would listen about the Hill of Gold on the distant plains of New Mexico. At last he wrote a long letter to the Viceroy, recounting his adventures and pleading for aid.

The appeal found a sympathetic ear. His Excellency summoned Bernardo to the palace, listened gravely to his words, and sent him on his way northward with a formal letter ordering all Spanish officials on the frontier to provide assistance.

21

Once again in Santa Fe, the dauntless soldier prepared to resume the treasure quest. With the renewed blessing of the governor, he set out with several companions for Comanche country. But now he could not find the Indians who had promised to guide him. For months he traveled here and there across the plains, picking up vague stories and nothing more.

The next year Bernardo came back anew, and the year after that, and the ones following. Each time, with unquenchable hope, he expected to find his Cerro de Oro somewhere beyond the horizon. It was the same dream of every man who ever searched for lost mines or buried treasure.

A footnote in one of the brittle documents still preserved in Santa Fe notes in passing that sometime before 1829 at an undisclosed location on the far plains, Sergeant Bernardo de Castro was killed by Apaches while seeking the Hill of Gold.

4

The Gold Nugget

Among New Mexico's early Hispanic pioneers, sources of entertainment were few. And most of those were improvised by the people themselves. One of the simplest pleasures, and one that could be enjoyed by all, was storytelling. Good stories were treasured and passed on from one generation to the next. Quite a number came from Spain with the first settlers—the ancient folk tales forming part of the heritage of all Hispanic peoples.

But another category of stories derived from unusual incidents or experiences in the daily life of the colonists themselves. They comprised sort of a running history of the humorous and tragic sides of existence on the raw, isolated New Mexican frontier. Many of the folk tales from Spain were long ago collected by scholars and published in thick volumes with academic footnotes. But unfortunately, most of the popular stories set in New Mexico were overlooked and became lost. Only now and then was one set down in writing.

It is those few earthy stories of the land, however, that I find the more interesting. They tell us something about the people and what mattered in their lives.

Poverty was an abiding fact of life during most of New Mexico's past, and, not surprising, stories about a poor fellow that became rich overnight were very popular. Even now, newspapers print accounts of million-dollar lottery winners or of people who inherit a fortune unexpectedly. They know there is an eager readership for such fare.

The Spanish New Mexicans had a number of stories about the lucky finders of gold nuggets, mainly in the Tuerto Mountains east of Albuquerque. The placer deposits in that area drew prospectors for many years, and a few did discover small lumps of pure gold.

My favorite tale of this type is the one about Juan Romero, a sheepherder. He cared for a flock of several thousand sheep, "on shares." That is, the animals belonged to a rich rancher in the Rio Grande Valley and Juan herded them for a year, collecting half the new lambs and half the wool for his effort. Once he was driving the flock with several of his young sons to a new pasture near the Tuertos. Suddenly, he came upon a chilling sight in the trail: an ox cart, the animals dead, and the bodies of a man and woman riddled with arrows. To Juan's experienced eye, this was clearly the work of Comanches.

Hastily, he and his sons dug shallow graves for the victims. Then, as the boys drove the flock ahead and Juan was about to follow them, he noticed movement under several sheepskins in the cart. Pulling them aside, he uncovered a trembling youngster of four. The boy, who only knew that his name was Francisquito (or

24

Drawn by R.H.Kern from a Sketch by E. M. Kern. P. S. Duval's Steam Lith. Press Philad

VIEW OF THE PLACER OR GOLD MOUNTAIN, AND SANDIA MOUNTAIN
from Santa Fé

Mountains where the gold nugget was found. Courtesy Marc Simmons Collection.

Quito, for short), had hidden during the attack that left his parents dead.

Juan Romero carried the orphan to his hut, and though he and his wife had many other mouths to feed, Quito was taken in, to become a member of the family. As the years crept by, Quito grew larger and stronger than his foster brothers. And he worked harder, perhaps to show his gratitude for having a home. During his little free time, he hiked up into the Tuertos to watch the placer miners. With shallow wooden trays, they were dry-panning dirt from the arroyo bottoms.

Sometimes the miners let the boy try his hand. Then, like as not, he would return home in the evening with fifty cents or more worth of gold flakes carried in a hollow goose quill.

When Quito was ten, disaster struck the Romero family. Juan, out with the flock on a winter's day, slipped on the ice and broke his hip. Borne home on a burro, he was patched up as best as folk medicine allowed. But it was clear he would be a cripple for life. From that day, everything went wrong. The valley rancher took back his flock, not willing to trust Juan's sons with its tending. Soon afterward, the eldest Romero boy was killed by Navajos on his way to a sheepherding job at Cubero, and another of the sons came down with a prolonged illness.

Had it not been for Quito, who now spent long hours at the placers, the family might have starved. Still, the paltry goldflakes he brought back in his quill barely kept them going. Every day, Quito began his hard labor with the hope that he might find a single big nugget that would lift the Romeros out of poverty and repay them for the kindness he had been shown.

One day from his bed, Juan Romero told Quito: "Go to my cousin and borrow his oxen. Then use them to drag logs down from the Tuertos. We are out of firewood." The boy drove the oxen into the mountains, where an early snow had covered the ground. As the animals walked, the wet snow caked in their feet and formed hard, sugarloaf lumps. As one of the lumps broke from a hind foot, Quito saw a familiar flash of color.

Excited beyond measure, he snatched up the snowball, and embedded in it was the largest nugget of pure gold he had ever seen. The Romeros' troubles were over.

But instantly a dark shadow fell across the lad, and he turned to behold Miguel, a huge and ugly bully from the mining camp. Quito was terror-stricken, and he tried to shove the precious nugget inside his shirt.

"What are you hiding there," demanded Miguel. But he didn't have to ask, for he had already caught sight of the yellow metal. "I'll have that bit of treasure from heaven for myself. Hand it over!"

Instead of complying, Quito bounded up the mountain like a deer. But long-legged Miguel was in hot pursuit. Finally, the boy was cornered by walls of rock that hemmed in an open shaft, abandoned long before by prospectors. Turning toward Miguel, he shouted, "This nugget is for Juan Romero." But before he could say more, his foot slipped and he tumbled backward into the dark mouth of the shaft.

Some miners working on the mountain above saw what happened and raced to the scene. At their approach, the rascally Miguel fled. The men sent one of their number down the shaft on a rawhide rope. On signal he was raised out again, the body of Quito slung over his shoulder.

The boy's neck was broken, but clenched tightly in his fist was the heavy gold nugget that, after all, would repay Juan Romero.

5

The Meaning of Gran Quivira

Since the days of Francisco Vásquez de Coronado, the word *Quivira* has occupied a special place in the vocabulary of the Southwest. To the early Spaniards, it meant "a land of great wealth" supposed to lie on the open plains far to the east of New Mexico. But later, Mexicans and Anglo Americans took Quivira to mean any "hidden treasure."

Curiously, the masculine form of the word *quiviro* has a different meaning in New Mexican Spanish: "brokenly"; as in the sentence *Habla español muy quiviro:* He speaks Spanish brokenly. But don't look for the word in any standard dictionary, for it is not used outside New Mexico.

The explorer Coronado first heard reference to Quivira when he stopped at Pecos pueblo in the spring of 1541. The Indians there had a slave who came from what is today Kansas. This slave the Spaniards called the Turk, because they thought "he looked like one." The Turk said his homeland was named Quivira and it was filled with gold and silver.

It is quite apparent that the slave had learned what these newcomers were interested in. By speaking of treasure, he rightly figured they would head east looking for it and take him along as guide. That would mean escape from slavery and a free ride home.

Coronado did push all the way into central Kansas, with the Turk every step of the way promising that unparalleled riches lay just beyond the next swell in the prairie. At the end of the trail, the Spaniards found only the grass houses of the Wichita Indians. The residents of Quivira were poorer than church mice.

The expedition's official scribe wrote that the Turk had told nothing but whopping lies about Quivira's treasure. Furious, Coronado had him executed by strangulation. Even though the vaunted wealth of Quivira had proved a pure fable, men still came to associate the term with lost gold. Sixty years later, when Juan de Oñate arrived in New Mexico to establish the first settlement, he too got the treasure bug. So off he went to Quivira, or Kansas, just on the chance that Coronado had missed something.

What is the origin or first meaning of Quivira? No one knows at this late date, but we can guess that it was an Indian word. Or perhaps, as one scholar has suggested, it comes from a phrase used by Coronado when he was following the Turk. He is supposed to have told his men: "*Quien vivirá, verá.*" Or, "he who lives will see," that is, will see what treasure is discovered. The soldiers contracted the words to form *Quivira.*

For the next two hundred years, Quivira was practically forgotten. Then about the middle of the last century, it

Coronado and his expedition were the first treasure hunters to seek Quivira. Courtesy Museum of New Mexico, neg. no. 20206.

obtained a new lease on life. Somehow, the word got attached to a large mission ruin about fifty miles southeast of Albuquerque, beyond the Manzano Mountains. Before it was abandoned in the 1670s, the mission had been known as Tabirá by the Spaniards. But Americans coming upon the site had no knowledge of its identity, and thought perhaps the huge shell of a building had been constructed by wandering Aztecs.

Benjamin Wilson, traveling east from Socorro in 1835, saw the ruin and wrote in his diary that it was named Gran Quivira. That mythical name alone was probably enough to start attracting fortune hunters. Ten years later, a New

Orleans newspaper reported that a group of Frenchmen, Americans, and Texans had gone west to seek the "treasure of La Gran Quivira."

In 1853, a military expedition camped briefly below the ruins. Sheepherders, grazing their flocks nearby, told the soldiers a legend—that at the time of the Pueblo Revolt of 1680 the padres had buried the gold and silver altar vessels outside the church and never came back to recover them.

That could not have happened since Tabirá is known to have been abandoned several years before the revolt. But still the fictional tale drew those hoping to get rich quick. Writer Charles Lummis, who visited there in the 1880s, said this: "Here is the asylum of the modern Quivira-myth; the Mecca of the Southwestern fortune-hunter; the field of the last folly. The Quivira of Coronado is forgotten, and in its stead is the Gran Quivira. It is no resurrection of the old myth, but the invention of a new."

And he added that so many people had come there to dig for treasure that it was not safe to walk about the place at night. One might easily fall into the holes and shafts that everywhere had been burrowed in the ground.

The search for riches, at least golden ones, came to an end in 1909 with creation of Gran Quivira National Monument. After that, digging was strictly of the archeological kind. Nevertheless, certain individuals in 1932 went to Santa Fe and tried to get a legislative appropriation to conduct a massive hunt for the treasure of Gran Quivira.

Legends, once they are born, seem to have long and durable lives.

6
Indian Treasure

To the Indian people of the Southwest, precious metals were more of a curse than a blessing. That was because the quest for gold and silver had first lured the Spaniards to the region. At least some of the Pueblos seem to have been familiar with gold. Placer gold, in the form of flakes and nuggets, could be picked up in a number of New Mexico's streams and arroyos. The Indians called it "seed of the sun" because of its bright color and sparkle.

The cacique, or religious leader, of Cochito Pueblo is said to have possessed a nice gold nugget that he used in a variety of sun ceremonies. But he was careful not to let the early Spaniards know about it.

Cochiti, located on the Rio Grande midway between Santa Fe and Albuquerque, still today has the legend of a village treasure which was hidden from the invaders and then lost. It is one of the few treasure tales I know that originated with the Indians and not the white man. According to village history, when Spanish settlers entered New Mexico they inquired of all the Pueblos whether they knew anything of the yellow metal. The Cochitis, like their neighbors, pretended ignorance and claimed they had never seen it before.

A padre came with soldiers and built a mission on the edge of the village. The cacique was unhappy about that. He told the people that the padre was there to take away their native religion, turn them all into witches, and steal their seed of the sun so that the sun ceremonies could not be held. With continued religious persecution, tension grew throughout the upper Rio Grande Valley. At last, in 1680, the Pueblos rebelled and drove the Spanish colonists

Pueblo Indians in front of their home. Courtesy Marc Simmons Collection.

and missionaries south to El Paso. But their troubles were not over.

In 1692, the Spaniards under Diego de Vargas marched upriver and retook the land. But the Cochitis were unwilling to give in without a fight.

Under orders of their leaders, they abandoned the village by the river and fled to the top of a high mesa a few miles to the west. They took with them, of course, all their turquoise, ceremonial objects, and the cacique's holy seed of the sun. Once on the mesa, they learned that a Spanish army under General Vargas was coming to defeat them. A council was called and great fear was expressed that if the fight were lost all the village treasure would fall into the hands of the enemy. So it was agreed that everything should be hidden.

Some of the elders wanted to stash the sacred articles in a cave. Others thought a better place would be under a large rock. Yet neither location seemed altogether safe. Finally, the cacique spoke. He suggested that he and his helper (the young man in training to succeed him) should descend at night to the canyon on the north and under the waters of the little stream that flowed there, they would bury the treasure. Since only the two of them would know the site, none of the other people could reveal it should they be captured and tortured by the Spaniards.

The plan was discussed and agreed upon. When it grew dark, the cacique and his young companion gathered up the seed of the sun and everything else of value. Walking down the steep trail into the canyon, they found a sandy place in the stream and buried the wealth of Cochiti. The rushing water quickly removed all trace of their work.

Next day, the Spaniards attacked with silk flags flying and trumpets blaring. The Cochitis resisted furiously, but their bows and arrows were no match for firearms. By day's end they surrendered. In counting their casualties, the Indians discovered to their dismay that both the cacique and his helper had died in the fray. To the shock of their battle defeat was added the grim realization that the precious treasure was lost.

Under direction of the Spaniards, the survivors returned to their village on the river and accepted once more the padre and his mission. The treasure left in the canyon was kept a secret from outsiders, but over the centuries that followed the village elders continued to search for it.

Only in the last generation or two has the quest been given up. The young Indians today—those who have heard the story—don't seem to think that it is worth the effort to go looking for a few paltry turquoises and a single seed of the sun. Those things belong to another age and are best left to the ghosts of the past.

7

Turquoise Has Played a Part

Sometime in the early 1530s, the wandering Spaniard Cabeza de Vaca passed through the vicinity of modern El Paso. Communicating with the local Indians by signs, he learned of an advanced people living along a great river to the north who had large towns, cotton clothes, and jewelry of blue stone. This was the first report of New Mexico's famous turquoise.

A decade later, Coronado found an abundance of turquoise ornaments among the Indians of Zuñi and Pecos pueblos. But the stone held little interest for him since he was intent on finding the fabled golden cities of Cibola. In fact, throughout the colonial years the Spanish settlers paid scant attention to the turquoise deposits that had been mined for centuries by the Indians.

For the Pueblo people, turquoise occupied a prominent place in their mythology, folklore, and religion. Wearing a charm made of this gem brought good luck and health. And bits of turquoise were one of the chief offerings left for the gods at sacred shrines.

We know that prehistoric peoples of the Southwest placed a high value on the stone. At the large ruin of Pueblo Bonito in northwestern New Mexico, archeologists unearthed thirty thousand turquoise beads in a single room. Small ornaments and beads were a major trade item, and turquoise specimens from New Mexico have been found as far away as Canada and southern Mexico. According to legend, the Aztec emperor Montezuma wore a necklace and pendants of the blue stone which had come from the Cerrillos mines south of Santa Fe.

Cerrillos turquoise has long been famous for its rich colors of blue and green. For centuries before the arrival of Coronado, Indians worked the mines with primitive stone tools. Over the years they removed more than 100,000 tons of waste rock. According to some scholars, the diggings in the Cerrillos Hills represent the oldest mine operation in North America.

In the late 1870s, Gov. Lew Wallace, best known for writing *Ben Hur*, began dabbling in mining properties, including those at Cerrillos. On a visit there, his wife Susan wrote an account of what they saw:

"We reached a turquoise cave and leaning over the edge, looked down and saw, not a narrow shaft, but half a mountain cut away. The mineral lay here which, through countless generations furnished the Indians with their most valued ornaments. The yawning pit is 200 feet deep and more than 300 in diameter.

"Thousands of tons of rock have been crushed from the solid mass and thrown up in a heap to form another

One of the old turquoise mines near Santa Fe. Courtesy Marc Simmons Collection.

mountain. When we consider all this digging, hewing, and hacking were done by hand labor alone, the enormity of the work is more impressive."

Some of these turquoise deposits were bought up in the 1890s by the Tiffany Company of New York, which invested thousands of dollars in the exploration and discovery of new veins. The company's mines bore such colorful and appropriate names as the Blue Bell, Morning Star, Blue Gem, and Sky Blue. One worker turned up a piece of solid turquoise the size of a pigeon's egg. Nicknamed "Jumbo," it was the largest pure stone ever found in the district. During the first seven years of operation, Tiffany's took out two million dollars worth of turquoise.

Other miners in the Cerrillos Hills made smaller profits. Most men worked their claims in complete secrecy, with armed guards to prevent entry of all outsiders. This was done partly to keep potential thieves from getting a look at the diggings. But it also helped in hoodwinking the tax collector. Much of the blue stone left New Mexico unreported, but officials intercepted one gunnysack containing 100,000 dollars worth of turquoise.

Several important turquoise mines were discovered and developed in southern New Mexico during the late nineteenth century, though none proved as rich as the Cerrillos district. One of these was the Jarilla Mine in western Otero County, about fifty miles northeast of El Paso. Another deposit, discovered by a hunter in 1875, was in the Burro Mountains south of Silver City.

By the time the boom in Indian turquoise jewelry came along in the 1960s, most of New Mexico's mines had been exhausted. To meet the demands of Indian craftsmen, large quantities of the stone had to be brought from other states, principally from Nevada, or imported from foreign sources. But to many people, New Mexico is still thought of as the land of turquoise. In recognition of that fact, the legislature in 1967 adopted turquoise as the state gem.

8
Quest for the Blue Mountains

Did you ever hear of the lost mines of the Sierra Azul? Don Diego de Vargas, governor of New Mexico and captain-general of His Majesty's troops, did. He went searching for them in 1692.

Sierra Azul means the "Blue Range." The name was known to the Spaniards of New Mexico as early as the 1660s. Governor Diego de Peñalosa, at that time, planned an expedition to the mountains because, as one of his officers wrote, "Ores from there have been assayed and are known to be rich in gold and silver." But no mention was made of the location of the Sierra Azul.

The Spanish colonists in the upper Rio Grande Valley seem to have been familiar with the range and visited it from time to time. Father Alonso de Posadas, in a report of 1686, referred to the Sierra Azul as a place famed far and wide for its wealth.

The first real notice the Spanish government took of the matter was in 1689. In that year, a man named Toribio de Huerta appeared in Spain and set before King Charles II an extraordinary proposal. He volunteered, at this own expense, to raise an army and go to the northern frontier of Mexico. His intention was to reconquer New Mexico, which had been lost to the Pueblo Indians in 1680, and, at the same time, find the Sierra Azul, said to be rich with silver and quicksilver. According to his statement, the Sierra was situated in the west, beyond the villages of the Zuñi and Hopi Indians.

Huerta claimed to have lived in New Mexico for forty years and performed all kinds of heroic deeds in the service of the king. As a reward for the new feat that he proposed, he asked to be made ruler over all the lands from El Paso to Taos, and to be given the noble title of marquis.

This strange proposal aroused the interest of the king, and he ordered an investigation to be made to see if the matter was worth pursuing. In short order, it was discovered that Huerta was a charlatan and a liar; his claim to valorous deeds in New Mexico was bogus.

The story about a legendary Sierra Azul, however, did seem to have some basis in fact. Stray reports in the government archives spoke of its wealth, especially of deposits of quicksilver. That reference, in particular, caught the attention of the government. In those days, quicksilver (mercury in its liquid form) was used in the refining process to separate silver from its ore. Colonial Mexico had plenty of silver mines, but the industry suffered because of the shortage of quicksilver. If a new source could be found in New Mexico, it would be of major economic importance to the colony.

Governor Diego de Vargas of New Mexico in 1692 searched for the legendary Sierra Azul. Courtesy Museum of New Mexico, neg. no. 11409.

In 1691 a letter was sent to Diego de Vargas, who was then at El Paso assembling soldiers for the reconquest of upper New Mexico. The message referred to rumors about a range of mountains in which a metallic substance or earth could be found. This material was used by the Indians as paint, by Spanish women to preserve the complexion, and by those suffering from smallpox to cover their scars. The substance was supposed to be heavier than lead, and so liquid and greasy that it could penetrate leather sacks in which it was carried, leaving red stains. All this suggested quicksilver.

De Vargas was ordered to interview some of the older New Mexican colonists to learn if any had actually visited the Sierra Azul and seen any mines. If the evidence for quicksilver or silver deposits seemed strong, then he was empowered to put together an expedition to search them out.

General De Vargas was delighted. This business of the Sierra Azul had stirred the interest of the government, which meant he would have an easier time getting supplies and support for his planned invasion of New Mexico.

Over several weeks he took formal statements from some of the prominent settlers who had fled from the north in 1680. They told what they knew of the Sierra Azul far to the west, and gave their opinions concerning the best way to get there.

The report of Sergeant Major Bartolomé Robledo was typical. He said that a red earth called *almagre* was used all over New Mexico by both Indians and Spaniards. It was greasy and heavy and made stains that could not even be removed with hot water. People found it especially helpful as a remedy for eye trouble.

His own father, Robledo declared, had gone many years before to the pueblos of the Zuñi and Hopi, bringing back sacks of the red earth. It had soaked through everything, coloring packsaddles, blankets, and mules. The mines, which he supposed were quicksilver, lay several hundred miles away and could best be reached by traveling directly from El Paso through a dry country inhabited by the fierce Apaches.

De Vargas assessed the information collected from Robledo and other persons, then decided that a search for the Sierra Azul would have to wait until he had reconquered and settled Santa Fe. In 1692 he marched up the Rio Grande, his army bristling with weapons, and in a few short weeks the old ruined capital of Santa Fe was again in Spanish hands.

With his base firmly established, General De Vargas rode west to the Hopi in hopes of getting a line on the red earth he had heard so much about. There, the Indians were questioned and their answers proved disappointing. The mines lay ten days farther on. The trail was steep and difficult with no water. Hostile tribes had to be passed the entire way.

That news was too much for the weary De Vargas and he returned to Santa Fe. But he did not go away empty handed. From the Hopis, he obtained samples of the red mineral which he later sent to Mexico City to be assayed. When the specimens were finally examined by experts, they turned out to be nothing more than red ochre or iron oxide, not quicksilver.

That disappointment quenched the enthusiasm of the Spanish government. No more official expeditions were launched to seek the Sierra Azul.

But the legend of the Blue Range with its hidden bonanza was not forgotten. For another hundred years, New Mexican colonists continued to scour the western wilderness on their own in hopes of making a strike. So far as we know, they never succeeded.

Many years later, in the land carved to form Arizona, American prospectors unearthed some of the richest and most spectacular mines in the United States. Perhaps one of them was in the mountains the Spaniards had known as the Sierra Azul, and the old stories were true after all.

9

Manzano's Mysterious Stranger

The little village of Manzano lies low on the timbered slopes of the Manzano Mountains, forty miles, as the crow flies, southeast of Albuquerque. It is a place where nothing ever happens—almost.

The name *Manzano*, which means "apple," derives from a nearby orchard, said to be the oldest in America. Local folk claim that it was planted by the Spanish padres sometime before 1676. Scholars believe that the apple trees date no earlier than 1800—but that still leaves them with a respectable age.

One spring day many, many years ago, a stranger came to Manzano. He was driving a team of sleek mules hitched to a wagon. As he pulled up in the dusty plaza and stepped to the ground, faces appeared at doorways and windows. Outsiders were a rarity, and this one was something special to behold. He stood well over six feet—tall and impressive. Adding to his kingly air was a wide-brimmed felt hat and a long frock coat of blue broadcloth. The buttons on the coat, made of gold coins, gleamed in the brilliant sunlight. The townsfolk gaped, open-mouthed.

To no one in particular, the stranger announced in a booming voice that he was the distinguished gentleman Don Tranquilino Romero y Aragon of Chihuahua. He was on a tour of the Southwestern United States to see the country and discover Spanish antiquities. And he would be pleased if the equally distinguished citizens of Manzano would come forward and point out the town's principal historical sites.

Curious now, people crowded around. Don Tranquilino pulled a bottle from his elegant coat and companionably passed it to some of the older men. The ice was broken and suddenly everyone wanted to be a friend of the newcomer. After a bit, Don Tranquilino asked to see the ancient church. The people led him to a small adobe chapel that was used for their weekly services. "No, no, not that," he said. "I mean the very old church built by the Spaniards."

"But, sir," replied the oldest man in the village, "there is no such ancient church here. A little south there are the ruins of Quarai and Abó, missions that the padres built for the Indians long ago. We have only this chapel."

"Ah, you are wrong there, my friend," Don Tranquilino said. "I have here an ancient map of this place which clearly shows a large church." And with a flourish, he pulled a folded piece of brown paper from his pocket. "Here is your orchard," he went on, pointing at the map. "And there you can see this plaza."

With long strides, Don Tranquilino began pacing off measurements shown on his map. Finally, he stopped and with an air of authority declared, "Let us dig here." Picks

Ruins of the old mission of Quarai, near Manzano, New Mexico. Courtesy Museum of New Mexico, neg. no. 6666.

and shovels were brought, work commenced, and within minutes the astonished townspeople had uncovered the corner of a building. Before the day was finished, they had laid bare the foundation of an old church and its altar.

Don Tranquilino was delighted, and he passed out silver coins to all who had helped with the project. "Amigos y compadres," he said, "we have made a wonderful discovery. Tonight we shall celebrate with a fiesta and music. I will buy the six fattest sheep in Manzano and supply all the wine you can drink." With that generous announcement, a loud cheer went up.

The fiesta in the dance hall was the grandest ever seen in Manzano. Young and old stuffed themselves on roast mutton and repeatedly filled their gourd cups with wine. By midnight the music had sputtered to a halt, and those merrymakers unable to stagger home fell asleep on benches or on the floor.

Don Tranquilino, who had eaten little and drunk less, looked at the snoring folk with satisfaction. Silently he left the room, closing the door behind him.

Next morning, the groggy residents of Manzano awoke and looked about for their rich friend. But Don Tranquilino, his blue coat, and his wagon and mules were gone. Not a trace could be found. Then a shout went up from one of the searchers at the site of the church foundation discovered the day before. Crowding close, the people observed that the stones of the altar had been torn up and a square hole dug underneath.

Examining the hole, they saw the remains of a rock vault and evidence that a square chest had been lifted from it. In the bottom was the fragment of a rusted lock. The men looked at one another sheepishly. All these years they had been sitting upon a treasure. And now it was gone, and they had been duped by the slick stranger from Chihuahua.

No further word was ever heard of Don Tranquilino Romero y Aragon, and no one ever knew exactly what he found under the altar. In the following years the Manzano folk spent many hours in hard labor, digging up the floors of the old Quarai and Abó missions. If there was more treasure to be had, no outsider was going to beat them to it. But for all their pains and calloused hands, they never found so much as a copper centavo.

10
Twists of Circumstance

Someone hides a treasure, cannot find the location again, and a search is launched that continues down through the years. Here is one of the most common themes associated with the large body of tales about lost riches. Such a thread is usually classed by folklorists as a "motif," which they define as "the smallest element in a story having the power to persist in tradition." The concealing of treasure and the loss of knowledge regarding its whereabouts thus become major narrative elements in these kinds of yarns. The three examples given here confirm that observation.

ARMIJO'S GOLD

This first tale concerns the father of Manuel Armijo, who served as the last governor of New Mexico under

Mexican rule. Manuel, after his fall from power in 1846, fled to Mexico where he was briefly imprisoned. Later, he returned to New Mexico and spent his last years on family properties at Lemitar, a village north of Socorro.

Sometime in the early part of the century, the father, Vicente, made a large sale of sheep and cattle, receiving gold coins in payment. Fearing that he might be robbed or that the provincial government might take a large part of the money for taxes, he determined to hide it. One pitch dark night, he went out on the plain with an old and beloved Indian servant whom he ordered to dig a large hole. At the bottom he placed his treasure, and then with great sorrow, so the story goes, he killed the servant and dumped his body into the excavation, on top of the gold. When he had replaced the dirt, he tamped it carefully to remove all traces of digging.

Still fearful that the hiding place might be discovered, Vicente Armijo the next morning drove a large flock of sheep back and forth over the site. So efficient was his concealment that he himself was never able to relocate the coins. For this reason, the son Manuel was forced to start life in very modest circumstances.

The whole account appears to be more legend than history. But local folks in Lemitar seem to have believed it because, until recently, they spent a lot of time trying to find Armijo's lost gold.

TREASURE MOUNTAIN

My second tale is about a treasure lost on a peak near the headwaters of the Rio Grande, not far north of the New Mexico line. Sometime in the early eighteenth century, a

Peaks such as this in Colorado's San Juan Mountains may hide lost mines. Courtesy Leslie Fishburn.

large expedition of Frenchmen from the Mississippi Valley visited the area. It was composed of skilled miners, mechanics, and common laborers. Close to what is today Wolf Creek Pass, they struck gold and went to work.

All summer long they engaged in placer mining, and as the yellow metal was collected, it was smelted into bars. The air was sweet and cool on the mountain, game was plentiful, and at first the Indians did not trouble the Frenchmen. Work seemed like play and the country like paradise.

By season's end some five million dollars in gold bars had been produced, and for safekeeping they were stashed in three separate vaults dug in the ground. Only officers of the expedition knew the locations, and these they plotted carefully on a map.

Then a series of misfortunes befell the party. Some kind of disease broke out and many perished. Others were killed in a raid when the Indians suddenly turned hostile. Only seventeen men of the original expedition got out of the mountains alive, and of those only two survived the journey across the plains. At a French trading post in the East, the pair of weakened survivors turned over their treasure map with instructions that it be sent to Paris. Shortly afterward, both men died from their ordeal.

The map made its way to France by some mysterious means and remained lost there for another 150 years. Finally, a man named LeBlanc discovered it and came to the Rockies hoping to find the hidden gold. He had no luck, being unfamiliar with the country. But a rancher named William Yule obtained a tracing of the map and got bitten by the treasure bug.

Yule enlisted the aid of several friends, and they began prowling the heights above the Rio Grande. Sure enough, the map led them to a series of old markings on rocks supposed to be keys pointing to the earth vaults. Eventually, a walled mineshaft was located and the hunters assumed it was part of the Frenchmen's operation. But the shaft was barren of treasure, and none of the vaults ever came to light.

To me, this story seems even more unlikely than that of Armijo's gold. But who can say? For the fact remains that one of the peaks overhanging Wolf Creek Pass is still called Treasure Mountain.

GARCÍA'S MISFORTUNE

In 1862, Don Felix García was among the most prosperous wool merchants in Albuquerque. On February 22, a rider dashed past his house shouting, "The Texans are coming!" These proved to be Gen. Henry Sibley's Confederate troops who, a few days before, had won the battle of Valverde south of Socorro.

There were no banks in the territory at this time, so Don Felix kept his money, mostly gold and silver coins, in a large trunk next to his bed. When he heard of the Confederate invasion, he decided he had better hide his valuables. Late at night, he loaded the money on a pack mule and sent his daughter and son-in-law to bury it in a safe place.

The couple rode quietly north to the little half-deserted settlement of Las Candelarias, above Albuquerque. There, in the ruins of an old house they buried Don Felix's wealth in the hearth of a corner fireplace. Several months afterward, when Sibley's army had been sent reeling downriver to El Paso, they returned, recovered the money, and brought it back to Don Felix. The incident convinced him that the trunk at his bedside was not safe. Therefore, he secretly hid the coins somewhere close by.

A few days later, he was sitting in his living room visiting with friends. Suddenly, the heavy dirt roof, which had been weakened by recent rains, gave way and crashed right over his chair. One of the poles supporting the ceiling broke, and the sharp end pierced Don Felix's skull.

The poor man lingered for days while his family hovered around. But since he never regained consciousness, he was unable to tell where he had buried his money. Finally, he died. For years, the García descendants searched for the lost treasure. They dug up the floors in the large house, one by one, and they plowed all the neighboring fields. But nothing was found.

Much later, Don Felix's property came into the possession of his grandson, Pedro C. García. For a brief period, he rented two rooms in a far wing of the house to a poor couple from Mexico. In an earlier day, the rooms had been used for storage. One afternoon, Pedro entered the apartment and found the woman plastering and whitewashing all the walls. He regarded it as strange that she would be putting so much effort into the project, but thought no more about it.

Two weeks later, the couple notified Pedro García that they were moving. Their reason was that the man had gotten a job on the south side of Albuquerque and that they planned to lease quarters nearer his work. Shortly, Pedro heard that the couple had built a new house and seemed to be unusually prosperous.

Had they found his grandfather's treasure, he wondered? Going to their old rooms, he chipped off all the new plaster. But there was no sign of any hole underneath where money might have been hidden.

So Pedro concluded that it was still lost somewhere on the place. For years, he and his children continued the search, but without success. Finally, the house was torn down and sold to make way for a new Albuquerque suburb. Perhaps today, in someone's front yard or under a city street, Don Felix's treasure lies secure, just where he left it.

11
A Silver Cache

Jesus M. Martínez was a Chihuahua merchant and freighter with plenty of nerve and trail savvy. In 1853, he led his own wagon train northward to El Paso and then ascended the Rio Grande to Santa Fe. But that was not his final destination.

From New Mexico's capital, he picked up the well-worn Santa Fe Trail leading eastward across the plains toward Kansas City. His intention was to purchase goods at the wholesale houses there and transport them back to Chihuahua. For his buying, Martínez carried with him twenty-one hide sacks, each containing 1,000 Mexican silver pesos. Since 17 pesos made a pound, the combined weight of the silver would have been 1,250 pounds. The train consisted of twelve wagons and twenty-five men. All went well as the party moved through eastern New Mexico, angled across the Oklahoma Panhandle, and continued to the Arkansas River in southwestern Kansas. One night, they camped on the banks of that stream and corraled the wagons.

After supper, the cook took a bucket and walked down to the water's edge to fill it. Soon he was back on the run, all excited. He'd spotted Indians on the far side of the river. At once, Martínez ordered trenches to be dug just outside the ring of wagons, and he placed extra men on guard duty. But the night passed quietly. Then, just as dawn was breaking, the dogs began to bark. The guards peering through the gloom caught sight of silent forms creeping through the tall grass, and they let loose a volley with their rifles. Instantly, the camp was on its feet.

The Indians leaped forward releasing a hail of arrows. The Mexicans stood firm and fired until their gun barrels grew hot. Finally, the attackers drew back out of range, carrying away their dead and wounded.

For four days the wagons remained encircled. Each morning the Indians renewed their assault, and each time they were repulsed. But the defenders paid a price, too. They had several wounded among them and, worse, they were running out of ammunition. As the situation looked hopeless, Martínez called a council. All agreed that in the dark of night, each man should attempt to escape and save himself. Before leaving, they toted the heavy bags of silver to a deep hole dug in the soft sand. Once the treasure was buried, they burned a campfire over the place to conceal all traces of an excavation. Then they stole away into the darkness.

The men hoped to slip undetected past the enemy and reach the shelter of sandhills north of the river. But unfortunately, the Indians seem to have been expecting some-

A typical wagon train on the Santa Fe Trail, after Gregg, 1844. Courtesy Marc Simmons Collection.

thing of the sort. One by one, they caught the fleeing Mexicans and killed them, some by torture.

Only Jesus Martínez managed to get away and he received a severe head wound. For days he wandered over the prairie, delirious and in great pain. At last, he was found by a Chihuahua-bound caravan returning from Missouri. He was placed in a wagon and weeks later arrived home.

But the ordeal had been too much for him and shortly afterward he died. He had had enough time, nevertheless, to relate the full story to his son. And as clearly as possible, he described the location of the buried silver.

Twenty years elapsed before the young Martínez was able to go and make a search. By that time the Indians were no longer a menace to the Santa Fe Trail. Also, Dodge City had appeared as a flourishing cowtown just a few miles east of the site of the massacre. The son easily located the right place. The ground was still littered with iron parts of the burned wagons and metal pieces of the harness. For two weeks he walked back and forth, digging and poking metal rods deep into the sand. But nothing was found and he gave up the search.

Before he left the area and returned to Mexico, the young man told several ranchers in the area what he had been up to. So word got around, and in the years that followed others came to try their luck at treasure hunting.

For those who may have doubted the truth of the tale, there were several bits of confirming evidence. For one, a Kansas City wholesaler named Richard Wilbur claimed that he had been the man who dealt with Jesus Martínez in the years before his fatal trip and that he always arrived from Mexico with huge bags of silver.

For another, Cheyenne and Kiowa warriors, after they had been confined to reservations, admitted having taken part in the massacre and looting of the Martínez train. Yet they always denied finding any silver. And then there were the remains of the wagons scattered in the river bottom, which passersby observed for many years. At last, someone from Dodge City came out, collected all the metal pieces, and hauled them away to be sold for junk. More recently, people with high-tech metal detectors have combed the area. So far as we know, they too failed to locate the missing treasure.

Old-timers believe that, because of its weight, the silver horde has sunk far down into the loose sand. If that is true, it may be a long day before any fortune hunter recovers it.

12

The Tucson Meteorite Anvil

I first heard of the Tucson meteorite anvil some years ago, when I was researching my book *Southwestern Colonial Ironwork*. Piecing its story together, I soon concluded that it was one of the most interesting relics ever found in the Southwest.

In February of 1851, a distinguished Philadelphia scientist, Dr. John LeConte, was passing through Tucson on his way east from California. The town was then within the boundaries of the Republic of Mexico. On his stopover, LeConte observed two large pieces of meteoric iron that had been pressed into service as anvils by local Mexican blacksmiths. As he later reported to a scientific conference in Albany, New York, his offer of a high price to break off samples from the meteorites was refused by the owners.

So far as we know, Dr. LeConte was the first person to take note of these curious objects and write about them.

But soon, other visitors to Tucson were asking to see the meteorites and they seem to have become something of a tourist attraction.

In 1852, for example, U.S. Commissioner John Russell Bartlett sketched the larger and more interesting of the two anvils, and included the drawing in the published report of his activities along the border. The sixteen-hundred-pound object was in the form of a flattened oval or donut; that is, there was a hole in the center. And the top, though containing waves and other irregularities, was sufficiently flat so that blacksmiths could use it as a working surface for hot iron brought from the forge.

Two years later, Lieutenant John G. Parke wrote about both anvils. The larger one was then installed in the Mexican presidio, or fort, and was being used by the garrison

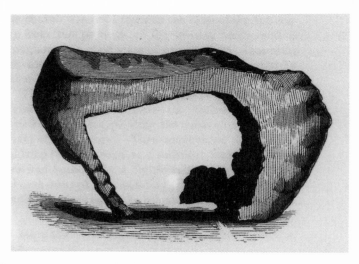

Tucson meteorite anvil, after Bartlett, 1854. Courtesy Marc Simmons Collection.

blacksmith. The smaller one, weighing about half as much as its companion, was located in front of the *alcalde*'s (mayor's) house, where presumably it was available for public use. The two, Lieutenant Parke learned, had been found about twenty-five miles south of Tucson, in a canyon containing many other meteor fragments.

It should be remembered that in 1853 the United States made the Gadsden Purchase, acquiring a large section of country in southwestern New Mexico as well as that part of southern Arizona lying below the Gila River. The survey and transfer of the land was not completed, however, until 1856.

Soon after that, Army Surgeon Dr. B. J. Irwin discovered the oval meteorite, abandoned and half buried in the dirt along one of Tucson's back streets. Taking possession, he announced plans to send it to Washington for placement in the Smithsonian Institution. Following delays and a long trip by sea and land, via the Isthmus of Panama, the "Tucson meteorite," as it was now officially known, reached its new home in the Smithsonian. Placed on display, it attracted large crowds.

The smaller of the anvil meteorites was discovered in Tucson by General James Carleton when, in 1862, he marched his famed California Column through Arizona and New Mexico in a campaign to repel Confederate invaders. Carleton shipped his find off to San Francisco, asking that it be placed upon the plaza "to remain for the inspection of the people and for examination by the youth of the city forever."

By the twentieth century, memory of the strange meteorite anvils faded. Then in the spring of 1976, the Smithsonian dug its example out of storage and shipped it back to Tucson for a brief exhibition. The occasion was the opening of the new Flandrau Planetarium at the University of Arizona. Dr. Richard R. Willey assumed custodianship of the anvil while it was in town.

On the afternoon of April 15, with the celebrated relic installed on the lawn of the planetarium, Thomas G. Bredlow, local blacksmith, set up a portable forge and lit a coal fire. He had been given permission to put the meteor anvil to actual use, something that had not been done for 125 years.

Although we knew a good deal about its history, no one could really say whether this outlandish looking chunk of iron was truly serviceable as an anvil. Could those early Mexican smiths hammer out a full range of products, or did the misshapen surface of the meteor severely limit what they were able to do? That's what this little experiment hoped to determine.

I can't imagine anyone better qualified than Tom Bredlow to have undertaken it. Having known him for many years, I can testify that he is a craftsman of the old school, of the kind that is nearly extinct today. I've seen him forge delicate roses of smoking metal and shape iron leaves and berries, exact to the last detail. Such work was fairly routine among master artisans of the Middle Ages, but not in modern America.

And what did Tom learn during the three hours or so he spent bent over the Smithsonian's prize artifact? The first thing he noticed, as he told me afterward, was that nothing had ever been done to alter the anvil's surface. There was no sign of rasp or grindstone marks that would suggest the original workers had attempted to improve the face of the meteor. "It was fine as a tool, just the way it had fallen from the sky," Tom said.

"A crisp new anvil straight from the foundry," he noted, "comes with edges sharp and square all around the face.

64

Before he can use it, the smith has to round off some of these edges so that in bending or shouldering the hot iron his work won't be distorted. But the surface of that meteor already had a variety of rounded edges, of different angles, just right for doing all kinds of jobs."

"But what about the bumps and dimples on the anvil face," I asked. "Wouldn't they cause problems and maybe leave marks on the surface of your work?"

"Yes, there are some difficulties there," Tom admitted, "but a good smith can aim and rotate his hot iron while hammering to avoid the hills and valleys. Even so, a few 'tracks' are likely to be imprinted on the final work. Yet, think of it. If some old forged pieces turn up in Tucson with similar marks on them, we'll know that they were made long ago on this very anvil. It's an exciting possibility."

As part of his experiment, Tom cut a section from an old iron wagon tire, straightened it, and welded up one end to form a country gate hinge, in the style of the Mexican smiths. Worn-out tires were a chief source of metal on the frontier. Going back to that traditional source, Tom explained, helped add authenticity to his project and put him in "a historical frame of mind."

Before the day was over, he made two iron bracelets, one for himself and one for Dr. Willey. He took pains to see that they were well marked with "tracks" from the anvil face to serve for all time as identifying hallmarks.

"That meteor can do everything a blacksmith needs it to," was Tom's conclusion. "I would like to have taken it home with me." And he added with a wry smile, "That hunk of iron was heaven-sent to be an anvil."

13

Did Ancient Europeans Wander the Southwest?

Once, while traveling in southwestern Colorado, I saw a curious story in a county newspaper. Seems some strange "writing" had been discovered on sandstone cliffs nearby. Experts from the Western Epigraphic Society had visited the site and proclaimed the marks to be of the ancient Gaelic alphabet dating back two thousand years.

Now, I had never heard of the Western Epigraphic Society, but the news story explained that its membership was composed of persons who had knowledge of the languages of antiquity in Europe. Further, they believe that in ancient times small groups of people from the Old World had reached the New, and in the course of their travels, they left examples of their writing carved in stone.

A good bit of this early-day graffiti has been found scattered around the Southwest. And, of course, it is associated with much controversy since professional archeologists generally dismiss it as the idle doodling of more recent Indians. But society scholars, said the newspaper, insisted that the new discovery in Colorado was genuine.

Gaelic writing, called Ogam, traces back to Ireland, Scotland, Spain, and even North Africa. The alphabet is composed of vertical lines attached by a long horizontal stemline. Each letter consists of one to five lines. A newspaper photo showed rows of straight scratch marks emblazoned on the cliff wall, and at first glance they might indeed appear to be Ogam.

However, I had seen marks like that before, and not too far away either. Some years earlier, I had gone backpacking through the Purgatory River canyon, which begins near Trinidad and angles down to La Junta, where it joins the Arkansas. Along the way, I spotted strange bundles of lines engraved upon the face of the canyon wall, and my first thought was they might be very old Indian petroglyphs or some unknown form of writing. At the time I had not heard of Ogam.

When I got home, I went rummaging through my library and soon came up with a likely solution to the mystery. It was in the travel journal of William Bell, an adventurous tourist who ascended the Purgatory Canyon in 1869, on his way to New Mexico.

"I found a place," he writes, "where Indians had left some grooves, made by sharpening the iron heads of their arrows." That explanation seems simple and obvious, and far more plausible than trying to make straight lines into some sort of mysterious alphabet.

Example of what some people believe to be Ogam writing, which is common in western Oklahoma and southeastern Colorado. Courtesy Leo Gamble.

It is not impossible, of course, that stray parties of ancient Egyptians, Romans, Greeks, or Irish monks did reach America's shores centuries ago. And if so, then at least some of the curious rock inscriptions found here and there around the country might actually be genuine.

One example that perhaps deserves a close look is carved on a lava boulder several miles west of Los Lunas in north-central New Mexico. Existence of this inscription has been known for more than a century.

In 1950, a Harvard scholar viewed the "writing" and pronounced the letters to be from the Phoenician-Greek alphabet. According to him, it represented a copy of the

Ten Commandments. He made no attempt to identify the scribe, or to explain how he happened to be in New Mexico, thousands of miles from home.

Dr. Frank C. Hibben of the University of New Mexico is also reported to have examined this mystery stone. He guessed that the letters might have been carved by Mormon pioneers moving west in the nineteenth century. I've heard that Mormon scholars afterward visited the site, but could come to no firm conclusions about the writing's origin or meaning.

More recently, a lady in Albuquerque, with experience in such things, has made a translation, or so she claims. According to her, the inscription was authored by a wandering Greek named Zakyneros. On the bleak face of this rock, he left a brief description of his journey. He also told of a companion who had met an "untimely death, stripped of flesh."

Unlike the straight lines I saw in Colorado, the markings here are quite certainly letters. But whether they represent the actual scribbling of some long-lost wayfarer, or an artfully contrived hoax, it is probably impossible to say.

The Southwest is rich in Indian rock art, the term now favored by archeologists to describe the numerous carvings and paintings on stone left by Native Americans. But that is easily distinguishable from the kind of inscription seen on the boulder near Las Lunas.

Someday, an absolutely authentic specimen of Old World writing from antiquity may be discovered in New Mexico. But until that occurs I, for one, will remain skeptical.

14
La Mina del Padre

The story of the Lost Padre Mine (La Mina del Padre) is one of the oldest and most persistent buried-treasure yarns to be found in the Southwest. The innumerable legends about this mine vary so widely in detail that it is practically impossible to sort them out and come up with anything like a reliable body of information.

Nevertheless, two "facts" occur in practically every version of the tale. One is that the Lost Padre Mine is located in the bare, brown Franklin Mountains above El Paso. And the second is that the entrance to the mine can be seen in the distance, at a certain time of day, from the belltower of Our Lady of Guadalupe Church in Juárez.

Accounts concerning the origin of the mine are conflicting. In some versions, it is actually a cave in which a colossal treasure was concealed. Aztecs fleeing Cortez's conquest of Mexico in 1519 are supposed to have stashed some of Montezuma's gold horde and jewels here; or again, it was Juan de Oñate, founder of New Mexico in 1598, who hid a kingly fortune in gold ingots and silver bars and never came back to reclaim them. Both of those stories are unarguably pure fiction.

So too, probably, is the tale that the treasure consists of golden and bejeweled church vessels brought down from Santa Fe and the missions of New Mexico at the time of the great Pueblo Revolt of 1680. A slightly different version credits the priests of Guadalupe Mission with working a fabulous gold mine across the Rio Grande, somewhere in the Franklins. Upon receiving word of the 1680 uprising, they hauled cart loads of gold, silver, and precious church orna-

Our Lady of Guadalupe Church in El Paso del Norte (today Ciudad Juárez), from the W. H. Emory Report, 1857. Courtesy Marc Simmons Collection.

71

ments to their mine and sealed the entrance for safekeeping. When the danger passed, they were unable to locate it again.

Many of the popular legends describe the mine as being a silver rather than a gold producer. According to one of those, a vein of metal stretched a mile in length and once yielded a single lump of pure silver that weighed in at twenty-seven hundred pounds.

Strangely, Jesuit missionaries are often said to be associated with the Mina del Padre. Fifty years ago, writer J. Frank Dobie reported that the Jesuits had secreted three hundred burro loads of silver bullion at the bottom of the mine shaft. Indians from Ysleta hauled red dirt dredged from the Rio Grande up the mountainside and filled the shaft with it.

The wandering Jesuit Padre LaRue is sometimes connected with this mine in the telling of the tale. But more commonly he is linked to the far-famed gold cache on Victorio Peak, one hundred miles to the north.

In any event, when references to Jesuits enter the picture, then doubt is immediately cast upon the story. The reason is that no members of that order served the churches and missions of New Mexico (which included El Paso) during the colonial era. The Franciscan Order had exclusive jurisdiction over the New Mexican province. Of course, that doesn't preclude the possibility that some stray or even renegade Jesuit might have found his way into the area and become entangled with a lost mine or buried treasure. But if that occurred, there's no authentic documentary record of it, at least not to my knowledge.

Other bits of folklore have become attached to the legend of the Mina del Padre. For example, over the years native residents of the El Paso Valley have reported seeing clusters of dancing lights on the slopes or in the canyons of the Franklins. Sometimes they are described as bobbing fireballs. In the Southwest, fireballs usually have something to do with witchcraft, but in this instance the lights are more often interpreted as being spirits who are standing guard over the mine.

Another folkloric element derives from Cheetwah, purported to have been chief of the Manso Indians, the tribe inhabiting the region when the Spaniards first arrived in the sixteenth century. Suffering under the yoke of their conquerors, Cheetwah led his people into the mountains where he summoned the aid of supernatural warriors from the underworld. Thereafter, the Mansos kept a watch over the high country to prevent Spaniards from desecrating it with their picks and shovels.

Chief Cheetwah, using magical powers, turned himself into stone so that he could stand perpetual guard over the Mina del Padre. Or else, the rock above the opening of the mine just weathered away naturally to create an image of Cheetwah's face. I have been told that if you know where to look on the mountain cliff, his face can be seen today from downtown El Paso.

Long ago, Dobie declared that he would not spend a single minute looking for the Mina del Padre. It was simply encumbered with too many implausibilities. Far more auspicious treasures awaited elsewhere, such as New Mexico's Lost Adams Diggings, and he would go in search of them, or at least their histories.

Others, however, have not been put off by the fanciful fables told about the mine. Legions of the hopeful have climbed the belfry of Guadalupe Church, taken their sight-ings, then scoured the mountains for any sign of gleaming rock or a tunnel entrance. Scattered amid the coarse grass, dagger plants, thorned brush, and cactus are innumerable test pits, some of them going back to colonial times, but others as fresh as yesterday. The legend of the Mina del Padre, it seems, will never be put to rest.

15
In the Shadow of the San Mateos

In west-central New Mexico, north of the town of Grants, rise the San Mateo Peaks, a range sacred to the Navajos and one rich in history. A central feature of this sierra is Mount Taylor, named for Mexican War hero and U.S. president Zachary Taylor, who died in office in 1850. It soars to an altitude of 11,300 feet and is plainly visible in Albuquerque, sixty-five miles to the east.

During the 1950s, prospectors with Geiger counters swarmed over the flanks of the San Mateos, looking for uranium. And they found it in abundance. In the ensuing boom, which lasted until the bust of the 1980s, little Grants called itself the uranium capital of the world.

The country thereabouts was wealthy in something else, too: treasure tales! Deep canyons, broken mesas, and steep-walled buttes, as well as the mountains themselves, offered a perfect landscape in which they could take root and flourish. And then there was El Malpais, Spanish for The Badlands, an eighty-four-thousand-acre lava field that spread over the desert south of the San Mateos like a huge dark stain upon the earth.

El Malpais resembles the Devil's workshop, with its cinder cones, lava tubes, natural caves, and hollows, and a surface so littered with sharpened rock that a hiker can have the toughest shoes cut to shreds in an hour's time. Still, this inhospitable volcanic terrain has had its uses through the years, mainly as a refuge for outlaws or Indian renegades, and as a peerless hiding place for riches illegally taken. If one believes the exaggerated accounts, then as much as half of the loot stolen by bandits from stagecoaches and trains in the old New Mexico Territory ended up sequestered in the labyrinths of these badlands.

Over west of the peaks, at a place first called Agua Azul and now known by the translation of that term, Bluewater, there comes a rather unusual treasure story. Late in the last century, a man named González rode up from his native Mexico and settled outside Agua Azul, where he built a small but comfortable adobe house. Inside, on one wall he constructed an uncommonly spacious fireplace and chimney.

Mr. González kept to himself, rarely making contact with his neighbors, who lived some distance away. A rumor circulated that he had been mixed up in the burglary of a cathedral somewhere in Old Mexico and had brought out a sizable quantity of loot. But since he lived quietly and poorly, most people put little faith in such gossip.

At length, González died and his house was left abandoned, since no one had any reason to claim it. Later, travelers camping in the area pulled timbers from the collapsing roof to use for firewood. That hastened the disintegration of the structure.

One day a local rancher was riding by, and out of curiosity he stopped and prowled around the ruin. He was surprised to see a tattered rag rope hanging inside the chimney. When he gave it a pull, chunks of adobe fell to the hearth and with them a roll of canvas. Upon opening the roll, he saw that it was a religious painting, very old and beautiful.

The rancher had no use for such things, but he carried it away as a souvenir. Later, he sold it for a couple of dollars. Some time afterward, word found its way back to Agua Azul that the painting had ended up in an Albuquerque art gallery and had been sold to a collector in the East for many thousands of dollars. That got people to remembering the story about González having looted a cathedral. But though they spent many hours in digging up the ground around his old home and even burrowing into the adobe walls, nothing more in the way of valuable religious artifacts was ever discovered.

Some time in the late 1960s, I think it was, I received a call from an acquaintance in Santa Fe who was a dealer in antiquities and western relics. It seems that he had been given, on consignment, part of a Spanish treasure that had been unearthed somewhere in the vicinity of the San Mateo Peaks. He had a half-dozen bars of gold and perhaps thirty or forty bars of silver. Before my friend put them up for sale on behalf of his client, he wanted to get them authenticated. And he asked me to stop by, have a look at the objects, and give an opinion as to their age and origin.

While I carefully explained to him that I was by no means an expert in the identification of such things, I would nevertheless be interested in seeing them. The "bars" turned out to be quite small and thin, approximately one inch wide and four inches long. They resembled in shape and size the little peanut log candy bars I used to eat as a kid. In the center of each was a crude but impressive seal that bore a similarity to the Spanish royal crest. The bars of silver were almost black with tarnish and felt quite heavy when weighed in the hand.

I said that the items looked genuine to me, about what I would expect to see if the ore had been treated in a primitive smelting operation and the metal, filled with impurities, cast into easily transportable bars. However, I suggested that the dealer ought to obtain additional opinions and I gave him the names of a metal sculptor, a blacksmith, and a metallurgist at Los Alamos Scientific Laboratory.

Subsequently, I heard that all the gold bars and many of the silver ones had been sold to a collector in New York. Of the history of this treasure, I could learn only that it was supposed to have been buried by a party of Spaniards coming out of the San Mateos, where they had been engaged in clandestine mining.

Such stories, as I indicated, are fairly common in that corner of New Mexico. But the one that immediately came to my mind in this connection was the tale called The Lost Gold of San Rafael (which is given in the chapter that follows). However, that tale has reference only to a horde of gold ingots and makes no reference to any silver. So, it appeared unlikely that the bars I had seen in Santa Fe were linked to the San Rafael legend.

The San Mateo Peaks. Courtesy Marc Simmons Collection.

More than fifteen years passed before I thought about this incident again. And what brought it to mind then was the arrest in Albuquerque of a scam artist, who was making fake artifacts in his basement, burying them at historic sites, and for a fee assisting gullible collectors to "find" them. He had been doing this for years, and rather skillfully so, with the result that the authenticity of nearly all historical relics found recently in the region was thrown into question.

Upon hearing the details of this neat little fraud, I wondered whether the con man, who eventually received a long prison sentence, had not known of buried-treasure legends in the San Mateos. If so, I suppose that without much effort he could have produced in his basement the rough little bars the size of peanut log candy and bearing a Spanish seal. But at this stage I had no way of uncovering the truth, and after all it remained possible that the small bars I had once seen and handled really were of gold and silver and, in fact, had been buried and lost long ago by a forgotten company of Spaniards.

16

The Lost Gold of San Rafael

❖

Ioften receive inquiries from around the country asking
for my help in the pursuit of some hidden Spanish
treasure. Generally, the parties want to know whether I
can direct them to a governmental or church archive that
might be holding early records or maps of use to fortune
hunters. In the main, I have to tell them that if such
material ever existed in public collections, it has long since
been stolen. After thirty years of working in Spanish archives, I can say that I've never encountered a single
treasure map or written directions to a hidden mine.

One day, I got a letter from a prestigious research corporation on the East Coast, seeking information about a
famous store of gold, supposedly buried on a mesa above
the village of San Rafael, west of Grants. The writer
wanted to know whether I had heard of this legend and,
if so, did I think there was any truth to it. The corporation

was considering sending someone to Mexico City to search the Franciscan archives there, since a padre of that order is associated with the San Rafael gold tale. Their research was on behalf of a client, who obviously had engaged a professional firm in hopes it could find a short cut to the gold. In my response, I was unable to offer much encouragement.

The basic outline of the San Rafael story is well known in central New Mexico. In a little valley that is bordered on the west by rocky mesas grading into the Zuñi Mountains can be found to this day a copious spring called the Ojo del Gallo. In 1862, the U.S. Army established here Old Fort Wingate, which was little more than a tent encampment. It was intended to serve as a base of operations for a forthcoming campaign to defeat and round up the neighboring Navajo Indians. Owing to the protection provided by the soldiers, Hispanic settlers arrived and commenced to farm small plots, using surplus water from the spring for irrigation.

The garrison was moved in 1868 some forty miles to the northwest, where it built New Fort Wingate. The people at the Ojo del Gallo were allowed to take possession of the old fort, upon whose grounds they founded the community of San Rafael. It is among their descendants that the memory of San Rafael's treasure has been preserved. Even today, some of the village residents continue to search for it.

The narrative begins not long after the great Pueblo Revolt of 1680, an event that witnessed the deaths of more than four hundred Spanish New Mexicans and sent the survivors in upper New Mexico fleeing down the Rio Grande to El Paso. They remained there, in exile, a good dozen years before the province could be reconquered. In the interval, a small company of Spaniards was outfitted and quietly sent northward

The modern village of San Rafael, New Mexico. Courtesy Marc Simmons Collection.

with instructions to slip into the San Mateo Mountains and bring out a fortune in gold ingots from a mining operation that had to be abandoned at the time of the revolt.

Leader of this daring venture, so the stories say, was a Franciscan padre. He was accompanied by seven soldiers, each stout-hearted and well armed. Using much stealth, the little party managed to reach the mine site and recover the concealed ingots of gold. It amounted to eighteen mule loads, wealth enough for any man, even a padre, to risk his life. When all was in readiness, they carefully removed every sign of their camp and activity and started for home.

83

After leaving the mountains, they made their first stop at the Ojo del Gallo because both water and grass were plentiful for the pack animals. Before the Spaniards could depart, however, they were surrounded and trapped by Indians. Whether they were Pueblos, Navajos, or Apaches has not been recorded; but whoever they were, their plain intent was to see that none of these foreigners got away alive.

The soldiers were seasoned hands, and under the brave leadership of the padre, they put up a stout resistance. Arrows filled the air and were answered by volleys of musket balls. But there was no protection near the spring, so the little band fought its way to the base of the adjacent mesa, where large boulders offered a natural fort. The padre, however, began to fear that their attackers might gain the summit of the mesa and shoot down upon them. So he ordered everyone to climb to the top, driving the mules in front.

During the ascent, one of the soldiers was killed by an arrow and two of his companions carried the body up the mesa. Unfortunately, the new position did little to assist the cause of the beleaguered men, principally owing to the lack of water up there. The padre called a council, and it was decided to bury the gold where they stood and then attempt to fight their way through the Indian lines.

Under the cover of darkness, they dug a shallow hole and buried the treasure, taking pains to leave no trace of their work. They also made a grave for the dead soldier, placing it about halfway between the mesa edge and the spot where the gold was planted. One of the men crept unseen down the slope they had clambered up earlier in the day, and he carved some signs in the rock to help them find this exact spot should they escape and later be able to return.

Freed now of the heavy gold, the Spaniards were far more mobile, and thus after dawn when making their break, they managed to get past the Indians. In the process, several of their number received wounds. Riding south, the party soon decided that they had shaken their pursuers. That proved to be a false hope, for after straying up a box canyon and being forced to retrace their trail, they fell into an ambush.

The padre and four of the company up front were promptly slain. The remaining two soldiers, riding at the rear with the loose mules, somehow succeeded in getting away. After suffering the most awful privations, they finally put in an appearance at El Paso and related the details of their disastrous expedition. Over the next century or so, two or perhaps three separate parties came north to the Ojo del Gallo, trying to locate the burial ground of the mule loads of gold. They found nothing. But the searchers did just enough talking so that the old story leaked out and became common knowledge among latter-day New Mexicans.

Since no documentary evidence exists to support any of this brief history, it might reasonably be dismissed as pure fiction—except for supporting physical evidence that comes from the mesa above San Rafael. Upon it, in 1935, a dying sheepherder from the village, Juan Alarid, claimed that he had discovered the padre's gold and had brought out a single ingot. He died before revealing the precise location, but among his possessions the ingot turned up, seemingly substantiating his story.

The ingot weighed about four pounds, and when tested it was shown to contain two-thirds gold and the remainder was silver and copper. That sort of mixture was typical when the Spaniards conducted their smelting under primitive conditions. At any rate, discovery of the ingot encouraged the folk of San Rafael to examine the mesa

San Rafael cemetery and the treasure mesa. Courtesy Marc Simmons Collection.

anew. Within a few weeks, they stumbled upon the grave of the Spanish soldier. His remains were brought down and reinterred in an unmarked grave, probably in the San Rafael cemetery, although no one now remembers the actual spot.

An ingot and a grave! Both things appear to affirm that, indeed, the lost gold of San Rafael was no figment of the imagination. And there is one more bit of evidence as well. Until recently, faint carvings could be seen upon the rocks behind the village, of the kind routinely used to mark the way to treasure. In fact, at least one is still barely visible. A discerning eye can yet make out the weak shadow of an arrow, pointing toward the rim of the mesa and perhaps to the Spanish gold that was hidden in haste more than three centuries ago.

17
Train Robbers' Loot

William T. Christian, alias "Black Jack," and his younger brother Robert were a pair who seemed born to a life of crime. After they killed a deputy sheriff in Oklahoma during the mid-1890s, they fled to the lawless New Mexico Territory. Here, they found three companions of similar ilk and formed an outlaw gang called the High Fives, after a popular card game of the day. One of the band was George Musgrave, a cold-blooded killer.

In the mayhem department, Will Christian, or Black Jack, was a standout. He led his gang in the robbing of trains, stagecoaches, stores, and post offices. U.S. Marshall Creighton Foraker of Santa Fe termed him "one of the most murderous desperadoes ever to defy Federal authority."

Maybe that was so, but it didn't necessarily mean that the High Fives grew rich from their crimes. The gang, in fact, seemed jinxed. Time and again they got little or nothing in their holdups.

For example, upon robbing the train station at Separ, a whistle stop on the main line between El Paso and Tucson, they came away with exactly 250 dollars. That was scarcely enough to keep a bandit in tobacco and bullets.

Along in 1897, a posse surrounded the High Fivers in the Animas Mountains near the Arizona line, and in the ensuing shoot-out two of the gang fell. But the Christian brothers and Musgrave got away, just barely.

That narrow squeak convinced Black Jack that their days as outlaws were numbered. Therefore, he planned one last try to rob a train, in hopes of getting traveling money that would see them safely to Mexico.

Late on a Saturday evening of November 6, the east-bound Santa Fe train pulled into the Grants station. A couple of passengers got off and one boarded. The engineer went to the loading dock, while the fireman, Henry Abel, remained in the cab. Suddenly, he was confronted by two men with revolvers and carrying rifles who ordered him to start up the engine.

About a mile out of town, the gunmen ordered Abel to stop while they disconnected the last half of the train. That left them with the engine, express car, and one passenger car. These they had the fireman move another two miles, where they halted.

Now, at gunpoint the fireman was led back to the locked door of the express car. That was quickly blown open by a charge of black powder. While the acrid smoke still hung thick in the air, the robbers told Henry Abel to go in first.

As he explained it later, the fireman thought his end had come. He was sure the express messenger, C. C. Lord, was waiting just inside the door and would cut loose with his shotgun at the first person who entered.

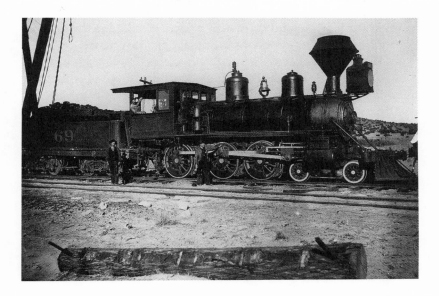

An engine like this one was held up by Black Jack Christian and his
gang. Courtesy Museum of New Mexico, neg. no. 44815.

But the fireman, to his surprise, found the car empty. It
turned out that the messenger had earlier slipped back to
the passenger car and hid out of fear that the bandits
would force him to open the safe.

They did not need his services, however, being well
supplied with powder. The planting of another charge
opened a ten-inch hole in the heavy steel Wells Fargo safe.
The eager robbers scooped out bundles of currency and
handfuls of gold and silver coins, which they deposited in
sugar sacks brought for that purpose.

Their work complete, one of the men fished a pint of
whiskey from his pocket and took a long swig before

handing the bottle to his accomplice. Then he thanked Henry Abel for his help and promised to mail him later a thousand dollars. As it happened, he wouldn't get the chance.

When the robbery was complete, the leader remarked to Abel: "If they want to know who did this, tell them it was Black Jack." Then he and his companion dropped off the car and started walking toward the lava beds. In the sacks slung over their shoulders, they carried off 100,000 dollars in loot.

A short distance from the tracks, the pair met a third man who was waiting with saddle horses and a pack mule loaded with food and whiskey. All three put spurs to their mounts and headed south, into the broken wilderness of the Malpais. Down near the far edge of the lava beds, they made camp in a remote hollow shaded by giant oaks and furnished with a spring of fresh water.

To celebrate their huge success, the robbers went to drinking. But as the alcohol took effect, they fell to quarreling. It was George Musgrave, we believe, who pulled his gun and in drunken anger shot Black Jack Christian in the head.

For reasons not clear, it appears that Musgrave and the slain leader's brother, Robert, then agreed to hide the bulky coins and currency in a crevice amid the lava, with the plan, no doubt, of returning for it after the furor over their crime had died down.

In fact, their holdup had thrown the territory into an uproar. The local press proclaimed it "the most successful robbery ever staged on the Santa Fe Railroad." A large posse assembled, composed of lawmen, agents for Wells Fargo and the railroad, and deputized citizens. But after chasing through the Malpais for several days, without being able to pick up the trail, it gave up and disbanded.

Months later, Pueblo Indians reported finding the remains of Black Jack, a bullet hole in his skull. At the time, however, nothing further could be learned about either the surviving outlaws or the whereabouts of the stolen money.

As is the case with so many western badmen, Black Jack Christian is reported to have been killed at other places, on other occasions. Thus, it is probably impossible to say with full confidence that he was the man shot through the head under the oaks in the lava beds.

What we do know is that Robert Christian and George Musgrave escaped into Chihuahua after the Grants train robbery. There, Robert vanished from history, while Musgrave, so records tell us, fled to South America, where he finally died in 1947.

And what about the train loot hidden in the lava crevice? Men have searched for it through the years, but to this moment no trace of the money has ever come to light. So perhaps it is still there, the location known only to pack rats and centipedes.

18
The Adams Diggings

The Southwest is rich in treasure stories, as any folklorist can tell you. But each state has a single tale that
shines brightly above the others, one around which a huge
literature has accumulated.

For Texas that would be the story of the San Saba Lost Mine,
sometimes referred to as the Jim Bowie Mine. In Arizona the
premier yarn concerns the Lost Dutchman Mine of the Super-
stition Mountains. In New Mexico, the winner hands down
would have to be the one about the Adams Diggings. Like all
such accounts, the facts surrounding the original event have
been mangled almost beyond recognition. Yet, through the
many versions there runs a persistent thread upon which a
storyteller can hang his hat and say, "Yes, behind all the
confusion lie hidden a few kernels of truth."

That master collector of Southwestern treasure tales, J.
Frank Dobie, spent the most time and effort in exploring

the history of the Adams Diggings. In the 1920s and 1930s, he would ride the train from San Antonio to El Paso and use that city as his headquarters in tracking down old-timers with firsthand knowledge of the matter.

Ultimately, Dobie published his gleanings in the book *Apache Gold and Yaqui Silver*. The material on the Adams Diggings took up the first half of that volume. Years later, when I did my own study, looking into old newspapers and other records, I found that Mr. Dobie had taken a hodgepodge of conflicting details and ironed them out to make a smooth and connected story.

That's what publishers demand and what readers want, so perhaps Dobie should not be faulted. This is merely to say that his account of the lost Adams gold should be read for entertainment and not taken as a reliable guide to launch a treasure hunt. Still, the best evidence points to the actual existence of a canyon laden with gold nuggets and placer flakes, found and then lost by Adams somewhere in far western New Mexico. That occurred in the early 1860s, when Apaches ruled that land unchallenged.

Adams, whose first name has been lost to history, was driving a freight wagon out of Tucson. After Apaches destroyed his wagon, he drove a dozen draft horses he'd saved to the nearby Pima Indian reservation to sell them. There, he met twenty prospectors led by John Brewer. This party had in tow a half-Indian guide, who, for a fee, promised to lead them to gold in a distant canyon. But they were short of horses and so showed considerable interest when Adams suddenly appeared with his twelve head.

Quickly, they struck a deal. Adams would join the enterprise, and in exchange for donating his animals he would share leadership with Brewer. Following their guide, the men traveled a week or more toward the northeast, skirting the White Mountains and entering western New Mexico. Finally, the guide paused and pointed to two mountains on the horizon shaped like sugar loaves, or *piloncillos*, that is, Mexican brown-sugar cones of the kind still sold today in supermarkets.

"The gold canyon lies at the foot of those peaks," he said.

The prospectors eagerly hurried forward and found the canyon within a few days. It was even richer than expected, with tiny nuggets everywhere in the streambed. By week's end, they collected a fortune. Inside a small cabin hastily thrown up, they put the gold in a deep metate, or corn-grinding basin, left by ancient Indians. For safekeeping, the metate was buried under a flat stone in the fireplace hearth.

When supplies ran low, Brewer took five men and pack animals and rode north to buy more at Old Fort Wingate, west of modern Grants. When his party failed to return, Adams went in search. Soon he discovered five bodies on the trail, slain by Apaches. Brewer's was not among them. Adams raced back toward camp, but too late. In the distance, he heard war whoops and screams. At that point, he turned and fled into the rocks.

Days later, Adams was picked up by a military patrol, wandering in the wilderness and out of his head. He babbled out his story, which seemed totally implausible to the soldiers. But a gold nugget he chanced to have in his pocket offered some confirmation of the tale.

Upon recovering from his ordeal, Adams lived in California. Years later, after the Apache wars ended, he led several expeditions of friends and investors in a bid to find the canyon and the metate filled with gold.

Dobie said that Adams had a terrible sense of direction, and after so many years his quest proved hopeless. But in

A pack train in western New Mexico that would have resembled the party of prospectors who found the Adams diggings. Note the Indian guide to the right. Photograph by Ben Wittick; courtesy Museum of New Mexico.

telling his story, he inspired many others to join the hunt. John Brewer, as it turned out, also survived the episode. He had escaped the Apaches by slipping into the rocks when his party was attacked. After losing his horse, he wandered for days in a starving condition. During one period, he lost his senses and walked along shouting, "Adams! Adams! My God what shall I do?"

By chance, he was found by some friendly Indians, undoubtedly from Zuñi pueblo. They fed and nursed him until he was able to travel. Eventually, Brewer reached the Rio Grande and encountered a mule train that took him to Santa Fe. "How glad I was when we rode in sight of that wonderful old city," he was to say later.

In time, John Brewer settled in Colorado, married an Indian woman, and they had a little girl. As the years passed, he kept thinking of the riches that lay buried in a metate under a flagstone hearth in New Mexico. Finally, in 1887, the year after the final Apache surrender, he loaded his family into a wagon and they commenced the long ride south.

One morning the Brewers showed up in Springerville, Arizona, not far west of the territorial line. John made some discreet inquiries about the nature of the country beyond, but it was not long before the nature of his business became known. Someone then informed him that an old man named Adams had also been in the region in recent years, conducting his own searches for a lost canyon. John Brewer was astounded. After a quarter-century, this was the first knowledge he had of another survivor among the original company of gold seekers. So far as we know, he and Adams never met again.

Brewer took several ranchers into his confidence, and over the next few years he led exploratory forays through the wilderness of mountains and plateaus. Always, he scanned the horizon hoping to discern the twin sugarloaf mountains that would point the way to the gold canyon. But never was he able to find those key landmarks, and thus his fond dream of relocating the metate with its treasure remained unfulfilled.

The separate stories told by Adams and Brewer, and handed down by an assortment of informants, contain numerous contradictions, as J. Frank Dobie discovered only too well. Yet the central thread remains intact, and unlike other such tales this one gives every indication of being grounded in fact. Perhaps that's what lends the story of the lost Adams Diggings its special appeal.

19
Salt on the Frontier

Salt has played an important part in the history and folk belief of the peoples of the Southwest. Besides being an essential item in the diet of both humans and animals, it is highly useful as a medicine and a food preservative. To the Indians of the area, salt had added significance as an ingredient in various rituals.

The mineral occurs in a natural and pure state only in a few places and usually in lakes. Because of the value of salt, bloody conflicts have often been fought over its possession. One of the most famous was the "Salt War" of 1877, a struggle over surface deposits east of El Paso.

The renowned Zuñi salt lake in western New Mexico has long been a source of supply for Indians of that region. One of Juan de Oñate's captains visited the lake in November of 1598 and reported that "nowhere in Christendom or elsewhere can such a marvelous thing be found. Not even our king possesses such salt." The Spaniards observed that the lake was covered with a hard, crystalized crust except in the center, where a clear deep spring bubbled forth. The borders of the spring were formed by the compact salt, as deep as a lance which the men thrust into the waters.

The Navajo believe that Salt Woman, a tribal goddess, lives in the Zuñi lake. People who go to gather salt from her home must be virtuous and without evil thoughts, so that what they collect will be clean and pure. Wicked persons, the Navajos say, can only find dirty salt. The belief that salt is a symbol of purity and has magical powers can be found worldwide. The Arabs, for example, burn salt before setting out on a journey to prevent bad luck. New Mexico's Pueblo Indians, even today, will cast a pinch of salt into the flames of the fireplace to protect the home and keep witches from coming down the chimney. Navajo tribesmen strew salt around their hogans, or houses, to scare witches away.

Because salt is necessary for life and is obtained through some difficulty, considerable worth has usually been placed upon it. In some parts of the world, it serves as money, and almost everywhere it is regarded as a valuable article of trade.

Bernardo López, Spanish governor of New Mexico in 1660, established a monopoly over the salt trade and made a handsome personal profit. Settlers and missionaries along the Rio Grande were forced to buy from him and at high prices. Not content with squeezing his own subjects, the governor soon expanded his business to include a yearly caravan sent to Parral, Chihuahua. There, New Mexico salt was sold to mine owners, who used it with mercury in extracting silver from ore.

Lumps of crystalized salt from the Zuni Salt Lake. Courtesy Marc Simmons Collection.

The best known and most abundant salt deposits in New Mexico are seventy small saline lakes located in the Estancia Valley, an hour's drive southeast of Albuquerque. They lie in a flat country between the Rio Grande and the Pecos River, which the Spaniards called El Llano de las Salinas, The Salt Lake Plain. After Governor López left office and his monopoly was extinguished in the mid-1660s, all New Mexicans had free access to the lakes.

In the fall of each year, the Spanish colonists made up special trains of carts and mules and went in a convoy to camp by the lakes and gather salt from their shores. Every family in the province tried to send at least one of its members, so as to share in the annual *cosecha*, or salt harvest.

Traveling by convoy was necessary since hostile Apache bands lived in the Sierra Blanca just south of the lakes. In 1730, raiders were so troublesome that salt gatherers from the area around Santa Fe were able to obtain an escort of soldiers to accompany them on their expedition.

The salt was carried home from the lakes in bags of leather or rough cloth. It came in pure lumps and had to be ground with a mortar and pestle for table use. Often, a medium-size lump was dropped whole into chile or stew and allowed to dissolve slowly. Many Indians still prefer this natural salt, when they can get it, saying that "store salt" is bitter.

In 1854, the territorial Legislature passed a law which declared, "All the salt lakes within this territory, and the salt which has accumulated on the shores thereof, shall be free to the citizens, and each one shall have power to collect salt on any occasion free from molestation or disturbance." Another part of the law made it a felony to interfere with any person gathering salt, or traveling to and from the salines. This measure, of course, merely legalized a long-established custom. Many visitors from afar were amazed to learn that the New Mexico government made no attempt to tax its salt, as was done nearly everywhere else in the world.

Even though the lakes were public property, from time to time unscrupulous individuals put forth bogus claims of private ownership. A New Mexican lady from an old family told me how her grandfather had been swindled. "He was well educated and a prominent rancher," she

101

said. "He should have known better. But when a man told him that he owned the salt lakes and would sell them cheap, Grandfather fell for it and came up with the money. Buying the salt lakes in those days was like buying the Brooklyn Bridge today," she added with a chuckle.

20

From a Prospector's Notebook

In the old days, the great mass of mountains covering a large section of southwestern New Mexico was known to Indian traders, ranchers, and prospectors simply as the Mogollons. Pronounced "Muggy-owns," the name derived from that of New Mexico's colonial governor, Juan Ignacio Flores Mogollon.

Today, this high country is encompassed within the Gila National Forest. But the sierras east of the Gila River have been given their own names: the Black Range and the Mimbres Mountains. Old-timers, however, still think of them as part of the Mogollons, which properly now applies only to the chains west of the Gila.

This corner of New Mexico was long the undisputed domain of the Apaches. In the 1800s, Spaniards from Chihuahua mined copper at Santa Rita, east of the later Silver City, but they always did so at the risk of their lives.

A primitive mine in the foothills of the Black Range. Photograph by Henry A. Schmidt; courtesy Museum of New Mexico.

American fur trappers came next, and they were followed after 1850 by prospectors who swarmed over the slopes and up the canyons of the Mogollons. From their gold and silver strikes sprang mining boomtowns like Chloride, Kingston, Hillsboro, Georgetown, Pinos Altos, Silver City, and the community of Mogollon.

For every story of a successful find and the booming of a town, there probably existed a dozen tales of discoveries that were somehow lost or "got away," like the proverbial big fish. From my own notebook, here are several brief accounts of treasures or mines that were reported to exist but were never found. They form part of the folklore of the Mogollons and, thus, are worth passing along.

The Warm Spring, or Ojo Caliente, band of Apaches lived on the east slope of the Black Range and in the gorges that threaded their way down to the Rio Grande, in the vicinity of the modern Truth or Consequences, New Mexico. Mr. and Mrs. Andrew Kelly were early ranchers in this country. They made friends with the wife of the band chief, Cuchillo, and did her a number of favors.

One day the wife asked Mrs. Kelly to accompany her on a trip into the mountains to collect herbs. Once there, she said she would reveal the location of a rich mine, where gold could be picked out of the soft rock with a pocket knife. Andrew Kelly asked why he couldn't go along, and the Indian woman replied that his presence would arouse the suspicion of the Apache men. They would then be followed and all killed.

When requested to indicate the direction where the gold lay, she pointed toward the mountains in the southwest and said they could go to the mine and return in three and a half days. But Mrs. Kelly was afraid to go, and so she declined. The Apache gold may still be there to this day.

In the same region, a few years later, a young man was working with a survey party running a line through the mountains. While out alone with his pack mule and equipment, he stopped at a spring. Noticing some bright-looking sand at the water's edge, he filled a sack with it and headed back to the base camp at Hillsboro. Soon afterward, he was stricken with an illness and died suddenly.

Among his possessions was the sack of sand. A prospector panned it out, and the return in gold flakes was enormous. Several eager parties went out in hopes of finding the spring, but their efforts were all fruitless. The young surveyor had gone to his death with no inkling of what he had found.

105

Another story concerns Charles W. Greene of Kansas City, who appeared at Santa Fe in 1884, making inquiries about a missing person. His cousin, it seems, had gone prospecting in the Mogollons two years before. From Socorro, where he had packed out to replenish supplies, the cousin mailed a letter to Greene back in Kansas, bragging that "he had found the richest gold mine in the world, located in the upper Mogollons."

In the letter, he told of blazing a mark on trees every two hundred yards for a distance of four miles, to aid him in relocating the mine site. And he closed by saying that when he next came for supplies he would send another letter, so that Greene could sell his printing business in Kansas City and come out to New Mexico and join in the mining venture.

"That was the last time," Charles Greene told his Santa Fe listeners, "that I ever heard from my cousin."

"Your relative is no doubt dead, killed by Chief Nana's Apaches who were raiding in the Mogollons in '82," responded Hon. Mike Cooney, Socorro's representative in the territorial legislature. Cooney himself had often prospected in that district.

And his guess was correct. Three years later, the bones of two mules and Greene's cousin were found in the mountains with arrows still in them. Searchers even came upon the trail of trees that had been blazed with a hatchet. But if the blazes truly led to "the richest gold mine in the world," no one to this day has ever found it.

21
The Ghosts of Kingston

Kingston may not be the largest ghost town in New Mexico, nor have the flashiest history. But its location, tucked in a narrow canyon on the east slope of the Black Range, has to be among the most scenic.

Little Percha Creek flows through town, adding much to its natural charm. The name *Percha*, local legend says, came from the fact that flocks of wild turkeys used to perch in trees along the banks. But the creek had its menacing aspect, too. Summer cloudbursts could send a wall of water tumbling down the canyon, threatening lives and property. When that occurred, daring horsemen dashed downstream just ahead of the cascade, warning residents at neighboring Hillsboro to race for high ground. Just a few years ago, Hillsboro was badly damaged by just such a disaster and several lives were lost.

In 1880, silver was discovered in the surrounding mountains, and two years later the townsite of Kingston was surveyed. The name derived from one of the nearby mines, the Iron King. Within six months of its platting, Kingston had eighteen hundred residents.

Like most New Mexico boomtowns, the place got off to a rocky start. Fast- riding, hard-drinking men appeared, on the lookout for a quick dollar. They were accompanied by speculators who hawked tiny lots on Main Street for the extravagant sum of five hundred dollars. For the first few months, Kingston was a tent city, with permanent buildings following at a slower pace.

Scalp-raising Apaches were also a threat, at least in the early years. Victorio's warriors lurked in the mountains, ready to fall upon careless travelers or miners. The first stone building in town, the Victorio Hotel, was named for the wily chief. It still stands, though no longer three stories as it originally was. Another fine stone structure, the Percha Bank, also remains. A registered historic site, it is one of the most interesting sights in Kingston today.

The man credited with making the first silver strike that led to the founding of the town was a whiskey-sotted old prospector from Leadville, Colorado. Jack Sheddon by name, he wandered one day into the Percha canyon, unpacked a jug from his burro, and drank himself into a stupor. Awakening late in the afternoon, he noticed the slanting sun striking a shiny boulder that had served as a pillow for his nap. Swinging his miner's pick, he chipped off a chunk of bornite, a rich silver ore. Then and there, he must have performed a little dance, for he had found enough wealth to pay his saloon bill for a dozen lifetimes.

Old Percha Bank building in the ghost town of Kingston, New Mexico.
Courtesy Marc Simmons Collection.

Sheddon staked a claim and called his mine "The Solitaire." When word got out, a rush followed and the land crawled with treasure seekers. The first notable event in the history of Kingston was a smallpox epidemic. The one physician in town, a Dr. Guthrie, converted a large tent into a hospital. Three ladies of the evening from the red-light district were enlisted as nurses. Victims of the epidemic, seven in all, were buried under the floor of the tent.

By the mid-1880s the population of Kingston had pushed upward to eight thousand people. In addition to stores and other businesses, twenty-two saloons lined the central street. There was a church as well, a forlorn symbol of respectability in an otherwise Godless mining camp. Funds for church construction had been raised by passing the hat among the many customers in the many barrooms. Coins and nuggets tossed in by the miners came to a hefty fifteen hundred dollars, quite enough for walls, a roof, and a steeple.

Like all such places in the New Mexico Territory, Kingston saw a whole string of newspapers come and go. One of the first was printed on a small press freighted up from Mesilla. Its enthusiastic editor urged readers from afar to hurry to Kingston if they wanted "to live long, be rich, healthy and happy." His was the age-old cry of the loyal town booster. Three later newspapers were *The Clipper*, *The Shaft*, and *The Sierra County Advocate*. Few issues survive, but those that do provide us with a glimpse into early-day life along Percha Creek. Especially useful are the advertisements for local merchants—the vendors of mining supplies, hardware, groceries, and leather goods.

It was activity at the mines, of course, that kept Kingston humming. Most had colorful names like the Calamity Jane, Kangaroo, Comstock, Little Jimmy, and Gray Eagle. By 1904 the district had yielded more than six million dollars worth of silver. Soon after, however, the price of silver declined, and that coupled with the depletion of the main lodes spelled doom for once-prosperous Kingston. Overnight, the population dropped to 150.

Fires have dealt harshly with old Kingston, and what was once a solid wall of false-fronted buildings is no more. Besides the bank and hotel, one can still view the assay office, a couple of fine residences, and the historic cemetery, whose graves were blasted from solid rock with dynamite.

It is an easy drive to Kingston, which some claim is still haunted by the ghosts of miners long dead.

22

New Mexico's Placers

O n the Southwestern frontier, every man interested in getting rich knew the meaning of the word *placers*. It referred to deposits of loose gold, mostly small particles, that had washed into streams from surrounding mountains.

A nice living, and sometimes even small fortunes, could be made by panning placer gold from the waterways. But the real strike came when a prospector was able to backtrack upstream and find the mother lode, that is, the source from which the placers had washed out originally.

A number of streams in northern New Mexico bear the name Placers, indicating that their gravels are gold producers. And in the last century, at least three New Mexico towns were called Placers, none of which are noted by T. M. Pearce in his reference book *New Mexico Place Names*. One community of Placers was located on the Rio Grande below Albuquerque. It evidently grew up when folks went to panning on the river bank. The Rio Grande, before damming, carried a good deal of gold. The nuggets and flakes were worn smooth, showing they had been carried and tumbled a long distance. This village of Placers was carried away in a flood sometime in the late nineteenth century, and today no one remembers it.

The second town by this name, usually termed Old Placers, is better known, at least by historians. It was located in the Ortiz Mountains of southern Santa Fe County, adjacent to deposits discovered in the 1820s. Lt. James W. Abert visited the place in 1846 and left us a description of what he saw. About two hundred people were at work here. "The houses," he says, "were the most miserable we had yet seen, and the inhabitants the most abject picture of squalid poverty, and yet the streets of the village are indeed paved with gold. All along the bottom of the stream and in the heart of the town you see holes scooped out by the gold diggers."

He also viewed some primitive ore crushers powered by a burro. People brought in chunks of ore, had it crushed, then panned out any gold. There was very little water in the Ortiz. Even today, the slopes are seamed mainly by dry arroyos. According to Lieutenant Abert, panning was concentrated in winter, when the workers could melt snow and use the water to wash the gravels.

They were too poor to own metal gold pans, so they made a wooden tray, called a *batea*, that served almost as well. Others, he tells us, used a hollow gourd or the horn of a mountain goat for the same purpose. When no water at all was available, placer gold could still be recovered here by dry panning. A few old-timers in the area use the technique to the present day. Sand and gravel from a stream bed is whirled in the bottom of the pan or tray, allowing the heavy gold particles to sink to the bottom. With a deft motion, rocks are flipped out, and soon only the finer material remains. Flakes of gold are lifted out with a moistened finger.

In the old days, this gold "dust" was kept in a turkey quill. A worker cut off the tip, filled the quill with loose gold, then reversed the tip and used it as a plug, which sealed neatly and tightly. Quills of gold dust were used as a medium of exchange in New Mexico, since coins of any kind were scarce. Some people even paid their church tithes with these quills. Larger ones held three to four ounces of gold.

A third town, called New Placers, to distinguish it from Old Placers, grew up south of the Ortiz, near the modern village of Golden. So much digging had gone on when Abert was there that he said it appeared to be inhabited by gigantic prairie dogs rather than humans.

After prospectors began scouring New Mexico's back-country in the 1860s and 1870s, other placers, as well as gold mines, came to light. Some of the richest were located in the mountains above Taos, at Hillsboro west of Truth or Consequences, and in the Pinos Altos district near Silver City. In September, 1882, a Las Cruces paper, The *Rio Grande Republican*, carried banner headlines of a purported strike in the nearby Organ Mountains. They read: "Gold! Organs to the Front. The Grandest Discovery Yet of Free Gold!"

Excited crowds gathered in the streets of Las Cruces to examine gold specimens brought in by the discoverers. The newspaper chortled: "Some of this gold, of course, will be sent to the Denver Exposition, and it will open the eyes of those who have said there was nothing in the Organs."

Bottles of placer gold recovered in 1915. Photograph by T. Harmon Parkhurst; courtesy Museum of New Mexico.

Contemporary mining records list thirty-three placer districts that have been worked in New Mexico over the past century and a half. But no Organ district appears among them, leading us to believe that Las Cruces residents of 1882, who let gold fever run away with them, ended up disappointed.

23
Treasures of the Pinos Altos

In southwestern New Mexico, just a short distance above Silver City, there sleeps the old mining camp of Pinos Altos. Taking its name from the "tall pines" that clothe the adjacent Pinos Altos Range, this nondescript little community possesses a history that is alive with treasure stories.

One of the oldest dates back to the Spanish colonial period. Not long after the opening of the nineteenth century, prospectors from northern Mexico discovered copper at Santa Rita, some dozen miles east of the future site of Pinos Altos. They built an adobe fortress as protection from the Indians, began taking out high-grade ore, and sent it on the backs of burros down to Janos in Chihuahua.

Someone from Santa Rita, a hunter perhaps, stumbled one day upon a glittering deposit of gold near the foot of the Pinos Altos Mountains. As the tale goes, the Spaniard in charge of the copper mine dispatched a priest and a gang of laborers to go and work the discovery.

In the space of a few weeks, the mining party emptied the small but rich deposit. Loading the gold upon pack animals, the men started toward Santa Rita. Halfway back, however, they were set upon by Apaches and took refuge on a mesa. The gold was buried for safety, but in the fighting that followed, all members of the company, including the priest, met their deaths.

Later, a search party found the remains and, by reading signs, pieced together the story. Much to its distress, the gold had been concealed so well that it was impossible to find. So this Golden Giant Treasure, as it became known in local legend, is believed to rest still in the underground vault where the doomed miners placed it.

American prospectors were the first to fully exploit the mineral resources of the Pinos Altos country. A band of them, led by Colonel Jacob Snively, arrived in 1860. He was an ex-officer from the army of the Republic of Texas who had made a name fifteen years earlier by raiding caravans on the Santa Fe Trail. Among the prospectors with Snively was a young man named Henry Birch. He knelt down to take a drink from Bear Creek, saw something flash, and discovered gold. The settlement that swiftly sprouted on the spot was first called Birchville, but soon changed its name to Pinos Altos.

Hostile Apaches swarmed over the land at that time, and numbers of miners took an arrow in the back. The danger did not dissuade Colonel Snively, nevertheless, from undertaking solitary prospecting expeditions. He ranged north and west of Pinos Altos, through the mountains to the upper reaches of the Gila River.

In an isolated canyon, he evidently struck a bonanza and began removing gold in quantity. Periodically, he would show up in Pinos Altos for supplies, and rumors circulated that he had a cabin and sluicebox at his secret camp. About 1865, the colonel rode into Pinos Altos one last time. He showed several friends a sack overflowing with nuggets, whose value he estimated at ten thousand dollars. Snively claimed that he now had enough money to set him up for life, and announced he would head for California to take his ease.

In fact, he turned up in Texas the following year and was virtually penniless. Whether he had lost his fortune in the

Main Street today in Pinos Altos, New Mexico. Courtesy Marc Simmons Collection.

119

interval, or it actually had never existed except in the minds of Pinos Altos gossipmongers is difficult to say. What can be verified is that mining men of that district remained convinced, for many years, that the colonel's gold canyon was real. And they exerted a great deal of effort in trying to track down the location of the so-called Snively Diggings.

Toward the end of the nineteenth century, but before the last Apaches were cleared out, a Pinos Altos prospector (some accounts say his name was Adams) went seeking the colonel's old campsite. Indians who had jumped the reservation ambushed and wounded him. It was a long trail back to town and the prospector traveled slowly, in great pain. At one point, he spied in the distance a rounded hill that seemed to have a reddish glow, owing to the carmine soil on its slopes. As he passed by, he discovered that the hill was liberally supplied with gold. Ignoring his hurts, he paused long enough to load his small knapsack to capacity with marble-size nuggets.

By the time he crawled into Pinos Altos, the game prospector was more dead than alive. The frustration of it all must have been hard to bear: the absolute knowledge that he had finally struck it rich, coupled with the realization that death was at hand. In his last moments, he opened the knapsack and poured out the bright yellow contents. "The Red Hill! The Red Hill!" were his final words. The incident threw the community into an uproar, and for months residents roamed the surrounding country keeping an eye peeled for any hill that might be tinged with red.

Proof that all of this truly happened resides in county court records of the period that show seven thousand dollars, from the sale of gold nuggets, was set aside for the prospector's next of kin, should any such person ever appear.

24
Boom Days in Mogollon

What's left of the old mining town of Mogollon—a jumble of stone and frame buildings—straggles along the canyon bottom of Silver Creek, in the mountains northwest of Silver City. In its heyday during the 1890s, it was a wild, noisy camp where burro trains loaded with ore constantly passed up main street, and bearded, be-grimed men wore six-guns on their hips.

A cavalry sergeant from Fort Bayard, James Cooney, made the first silver strike in the early 1870s. His plan was to pile up a fortune, then go back East to marry his sweet-heart. But Apaches jumped him on his claim one day, and that was the end of Sergeant Cooney and his rosy dream.

But where he had led, others soon followed. As the Indians were pushed onto reservations, prospectors swarmed through the Gila country. Many of them found promising mineral outcrops in the vicinity of Silver Creek, and about 1889 the first cabin was raised on the site of Mogollon. Saloons, stores, a blacksmith shop, livery stables, post office, and homes mushroomed.

One early saloon was graced with the unlikely name, "The Bloated Goat." Local tradition has it that as the building was going up, the proprietor asked a cowboy, known for his artistic ability, to draw a sketch of a steer, which could serve as a model for a painting on the saloon wall. Flattered, the cowboy produced a rough drawing. One salty prospector who saw it exclaimed, "Oh, my God! It looks like a bloated goat." So the saloon had a new name, but it never did get the painting of a steer.

Mogollon, like most of New Mexico's mining camps, had its full share of lawlessness. The notorious Butch Cassidy is reputed to have committed several holdups and murders in the area. Two bandits once robbed the Mogollon Mercantile Company, which was keeping the mine payroll in its safe. The pair mercilessly gunned down the manager and clerk, grabbed the money, and fled to the hills. Men in nearby saloons heard the shooting, but thought it was shutters banging in the wind. A posse mounted up and pursued the culprits into the hills, where one was killed and the other captured.

In December 1912, a band of outlaws held up the Silver City and Mogollon Stage Line, getting away with the strongbox. Passengers on the coach were able to give a good description of the thieves. That led to the arrest of three prominent merchants in the neighboring town of Alma and of one of Mogollon's own deputies. The scandal rocked the two small communities.

But all was not murder and mayhem among the miners. As was the case on much of the American frontier, there

Mogollon after the mining boom ended. Courtesy State Records Center and Archives, Lucian File Collection #12772.

existed a strong element in favor of calm, order, and the development of civilized institutions.

Churches and schools flourished from Mogollon's earliest days. One writer in 1911 noted with pride: "The population, numbering 1,800, is composed of people representing every state in the United States, and in point of average culture, refinement, and education compare favorably with the centers of civilization and intelligence in the cities of the East. The young men are temperate in their habits, gentlemanly in their deportment, and the community as a whole are law abiding citizens."

The mines, both silver and gold, gave life to Mogollon. Operations like the Little Fannie, Maud S, Deep Down, and the Last Chance eventually yielded some twenty million dollars in ore. But mining booms are always of limited duration. As the rich metal was exhausted, Mogollon began to wither. By 1930 the town's population had dropped to two hundred. The last mine closed in the 1950s.

Today, Mogollon is drowsy but not dead. Shops and galleries occupy the old buildings and summer visitors prowl about the deserted mines, where a bit of New Mexico history is still preserved. For those seeking a remnant of the Old West, Mogollon has plenty to offer.

25

The German's Knapsack

Old Fort Cummings was built by the U.S. Army in 1863 to protect the main stage road that ran between El Paso and Tucson from roving Apaches. The post was located above today's town of Deming and faced north to the bald knob of Cooke's Peak and the ridges of purple mountains that rose beyond it. On a bracing fall day in 1872, the commander of Fort Cummings decided to send a wood-cutting party into the high country to begin gathering fuel needed to heat the barracks and officers' quarters through the winter. The commander, a Captain Tucker, placed one of his trusted noncoms, an Irish sergeant named McGurk, in charge of the detail.

The sergeant, a member in C Company of the Fourth Regiment, was allowed to select ten troopers to serve as an escort and guard for the civilian wood cutters. He chose five green rookies and five older veterans, pairing them up. Explaining, he said: "My experience was that the rookies are anxious and willing to do what they are told, while the vets prefer to play cards and sleep while on these details. The eager boys help keep the vets on their toes."

Jake Schaeffer, a German, was picked by Sergeant McGurk to act as cook for the party. It was a popular belief among frontiersmen that all Germans were good cooks, but also that they were of no use in the forest. Invariably, they would lose their bearings the minute they were out of sight of camp and someone would have to retrieve them. It was because Schaeffer lacked any sense of direction that he became the chief figure in this story.

Another man was added to the crew, Mr. Young, who was a blacksmith taken to keep the horses and mules shod. He owned a shepherd dog used by the soldiers at the fort to herd their horses, and he received permission to have this animal accompany him on the trip. The dog could serve as a sentinel, since Captain Tucker had warned that Chief Victorio and his renegade Apaches were on the loose and might cause trouble. The work crew and its escort marched out of Fort Cummings and headed northward into the mountains near the headwaters of the Mimbres River. At a well-timbered spot, camp was pitched and the men broke out their axes and saws.

Over the next couple of weeks, the piles of wood grew shoulder-high, ready to be carted back to the fort. Mr. Young, doubling as hunter, found game plentiful and kept the hungry men well supplied with fresh meat. During evenings around the campfire, the tired crew smoked, sang, and told tales. It was a pleasant interlude for all, before winter's cold came creeping down from the mountaintops.

Ruins of old Fort Cummings, New Mexico, and Cooke's Peak in the distance. Courtesy Marc Simmons Collection.

One morning, as Young prepared to set out on a hunt, the German cook asked Sergeant McGurk for permission to go along. He explained that he had never shot a deer in his life, and this was a first-rate opportunity. When asked his opinion, Mr. Young replied, "Sure! Give him his chance. I'll take care of him."

127

Sergeant McGurk carefully supervised Jake's preparations. He had the German take a carbine and extra cartridges and helped fill his knapsack with hardtack, the wheat crackers that fed soldiers through the Civil War and the Indian wars. Last, he warned him to keep his canteen full at all times, to avoid running out of water.

Confidently, McGurk bid his cook good-bye. As he would tell it long afterward: "That was the last I saw of Jake for three months." Late the same afternoon, hunter Young arrived back in camp all crestfallen, saying that he had lost the German. They had separated and he heard him fire his rifle, and supposed that Jake had gone in pursuit of a wounded deer. But in spite of a diligent search, he had not been able to find him.

The sergeant stuffed some food in his saddlebags, and the two men, followed by Young's dog, went looking. They reached the spot where Jake had last been seen, and soon discovered his tracks following the bloody trail of a deer. Rifles fired in the air brought no response. The dog led them to the dead deer, but the cook was nowhere to be found.

The pair off-saddled, hobbled their horses and turned them loose, then built a fire and roasted some of the venison. They planned to sleep and at daylight start out again. But the dog kept waking them by licking their faces and growling, as if afraid. Something out in the darkness was making him uneasy. An hour before sunup, Mr. Young, worried now, sent the dog out to drive in the horses, but the poor beast didn't want to go. He betrayed a mournful look and whined pitifully, but finally left on his errand. As McGurk related it, "We never saw that dog or our horses again."

In a half-hour, Young whispered that it was time to clear out of there. "We're surrounded by Apaches," he declared. As they hurried away, he added, "McGurk, I don't believe they'll get us this time, unless they are hiding in that bunch of aspen over yonder." In that instant, a cloud of arrows assailed them from the grove. One struck Young in the head, piercing his brain. The sergeant, fleet of foot, escaped and managed to reach camp. There, however, another shock greeted him. The Indians had raided, killing all the wood choppers, two of the soldiers, and carrying away the entire horseherd. McGurk gathered the survivors, and they hiked back to Fort Cummings to report the disaster.

Captain Tucker at once designated a small guard to remain on duty at the post, and taking the remainder of the troopers, including Sergeant McGurk, he rode to the wood camp to bury the dead. With that grisly chore completed, he and his men commenced following the broad trail of the Apache marauders. It led northward through the Black Range, then along the edge of the sweeping San Agustín Plains, around the Datil Mountains, and finally pointed south again, where it eventually disappeared across the Mexican border.

Having made a wide and fruitless circle, the frustrated Captain Tucker guided his little expedition back to the wood camp and supervised removal of the cut timber to Fort Cummings. In all of their wanderings, the men had discovered no trace of the missing German, Jake Schaeffer. Had the Indians killed him, or had he merely wandered lost until starvation at last claimed him?

The mystery was resolved a month later when a patrol passed through from Fort Craig, a garrison on the Rio Grande one hundred miles to the northeast. The German had drifted into Craig, the dusty soldiers declared; he was barefoot, without his rifle, and clutching his knapsack with a death grip. He was wild-eyed and crazy as a loon, and he kept muttering the name of Young.

Some of the troops at Fort Craig did get a quick look inside the knapsack. It was filled with pure gold nuggets, upward of ten pounds or so. The German abruptly closed the flap, and in a twinkle he raced from the fort on foot and headed for the brushy banks of the Rio Grande a mile away. Before the soldiers recovered from their surprise, he had disappeared.

A detail dispatched in pursuit found him near a Mexican hut, stark naked and the knapsack nowhere in sight. Had he thrown his clothes and gold into the river, or had they been stolen? Poor Schaeffer was so far gone that he could not give an answer. Returned to the post hospital, he hovered near death for days. Then he began a slow improvement. Upon being questioned, the German had only a faint memory of his experience. He recalled shooting the deer and getting lost as he tried to follow it. But where the gold nuggets came from, he had no idea, or so he said. One dim recollection remained of crossing a broad plain grazed by bands of antelope and seeing on its far edge a rising mountain with the image of a woman's face on its upper slope.

Upon recovering well enough to travel, Schaeffer made his way back to Fort Cummings. But his old companions there noted a marked change in him. "He was never again like his old self," observed Sergeant McGurk. "He would leave the fort and be gone for days, always returning glum and empty-handed." We must assume, of course, that Jake Schaeffer was nosing about in hopes of finding the source of the gold nuggets.

Sergeant McGurk had something similar in mind. When he was mustered out of the army the following August, he laid plans to make his own prospecting excursion in search of what he now called "Schaeffer's Diggin's." And he had fashioned some general notion of where the gold ought to be. Since he had loaded the German's knapsack with hardtack, he reasoned, the man being lost wouldn't have thrown away food even to replace it with nuggets. So the gold must have been found toward the end of Jake's wanderings, after he had consumed all or most of the crackers. The antelope probably were seen on the San Agustín Plains, where they are common, even today. And the clincher? Just beyond the plains towered the Magdalena Mountains, supposedly named by Spaniards for Mary Magdalene, the outline of whose face is formed by rocks near the summit of the north peak.

Before initiating his effort to locate Schaeffer's Diggin's, McGurk traveled to his original home in Columbus, Ohio, on a visit. There, far from the deserts of the Southwest, his plan of prospecting for gold, with its attendant hardships and dangers, no longer seemed so attractive. Thus, when his path chanced to cross that of an army recruiter, he signed up for another hitch and his treasure hunt never came about.

As for Jake Schaeffer, who made an ever so brief entry onto the pages of history, he swiftly vanished from view, as poor, we must assume, as when he first appeared in the records of old Fort Cummings.

26
Lost Gold, Found?

One day, I received an electrifying telegram from my friend Paul Bentrup in Kansas. According to his brief message, a story I had sent to the *Hugoton Hermes,* a local paper, about buried gold at Flag Spring in the nearby Oklahoma Panhandle had set off a treasure hunt, with spectacular results.

Three residents of Hugoton, including the town druggist, had seen my account and its accompanying map. On a weekend, they loaded up gear and a metal detector and headed south across the state line. The next thing anyone knew, the trio had returned home with a startling announcement. They had struck it rich, digging up ingots of pure gold worth several million dollars. People dropping by the drug store were given a look, and a man from the IRS even came to town to be sure that Uncle Sam got his share.

As the news spread, southwestern Kansas was thrown into an uproar. Not much happens in that corner of the country, and a story like this quickened the blood of normally calm farming and ranching folk. In the excitement, some people visited the hardware store to buy picks and shovels, intending to search for any gold that might have been overlooked.

The tale of lost treasure that I had sent over to Hugoton was like a thousand other such yarns common in the Southwest—more fiction probably than fact. I certainly hadn't expected it to launch a modern-day gold rush. The origins of the whole business date back to 1802, when a band of thirteen French adventurers, among them a defrocked priest named Pierre LaFarge, left New Orleans by ship for the Mexican port of Matamoros. After landing, they made their way overland to Chihuahua and engaged in a bit of highway banditry.

When things got too hot in Chihuahua, the gang fled north to El Paso and then continued on to Santa Fe and Taos. After several episodes of troublemaking in these towns, they moved to the Moreno Valley in the mountains east of Taos. There, Spaniards were taking placer gold from the streams. For a year the Frenchmen also panned for gold, but the work was hard. So they turned to robbing and killing others, until they had accumulated a large quantity of dust and flakes. Six of the party were killed in the course of the crime spree. The seven survivors finally decided it was time to get out of New Mexico with their treasure and return across country to New Orleans.

One of their number went to Santa Fe and hired a Spaniard named José Lopat to come to the Moreno Valley and melt down the gold into ingots. Lopat, who had experience in metallurgy, built a small furnace and pro-

Sugarloaf Mountain in the Oklahoma Panhandle, a central landmark in the search for lost gold. Courtesy Marc Simmons Collection.

duced five hundred ingots weighing just over seven pounds each. Then he was enlisted to guide the men eastward.

Soon after crossing the present-day boundary of New Mexico, the party encamped at Flag Spring. Two American trappers on their way to the Rockies wandered in and imparted startling news. The United States had recently completed the Louisiana Purchase with Napoleon, so that New Orleans no longer belonged to France! The Frenchmen were dismayed. If they returned home, they feared the new government would confiscate their gold.

Two of the men were sent ahead at once to check out the situation in New Orleans, and see if it would be possible to ship the treasure through to France. The remainder agreed to wait three months at Flag Spring. If they received no word, they would bury the gold and continue on to Louisiana themselves. At this point, José Lopat was sent back to Santa Fe. He heard no more of the matter for a couple of years, and then the ex-priest Pierre LaFarge appeared in the capital. He was suffering from advanced tuberculosis, and he had returned to Santa Fe in hopes that the thin air would help his lungs.

From LaFarge, José learned that all the other Frenchmen had been killed, either by Indians or in barroom fights, when they reached New Orleans. They had indeed buried all their gold near Flag Spring and none had been able to return for it.

LaFarge soon died from his ailment, so that José Lopat was the only man left who knew the story. Once, in later years, he returned to the spring to search. But he lacked directions or a map, and the country was so large that he had no hope of actually finding the gold. Late in life, José gave a full account of the episode to his son Emanuel, who wrote it all down on the flyleaves of a family Bible. Angelina Lopat, a granddaughter, inherited the book and kept it until her death at Denver in 1925, at age eighty-seven. It was she who told the story to others.

In her many tellings, the gold was always located in the vicinity of Flag Spring, a major landmark on the old Santa Fe Trail. The earliest traders on the trail had initially called the site Upper Spring. Since it was a half-mile or so north of the main trail, somebody raised a tall pole and tied a white rag to it as a marker. After that, the name Flag Spring came into common use.

Even before Angelina Lopat began spinning her tale, rumors of hidden gold circulated in Oklahoma's westernmost county, Cimarron County, where lay the spring. Mike Ryan, an old freighter on the trail in the 1860s and 1870s, came back and burrowed a cluster of holes and tunnels all around the small pool of water, without uncovering any clues. Then, toward the end of the last century, a startling find was made. Some cowboys discovered three Roman numerals, each many yards long, that had been formed by burying stones in the sandy prairie and leaving their surfaces exposed. The numbers were I, IV, and V, and had been placed approximately six miles apart, seemingly to form a triangle. Speculation immediately arose, of course, that the numerals represented some sort of marking devices left by the original Frenchmen, to serve them as aids in recovering their treasure. But how were they to be interpreted? No one seemed to know, although guesses flew as thick as crows in a cornfield.

Finally, a couple of decades ago, a rancher on horseback stumbled upon a fourth numeral, IX, and matters came into sharper focus. With this number now, an almost perfect square could be plotted, its sides each six miles square (encompassing thirty-six square miles) and with a numeral anchoring each corner. Drawing two diagonal lines from opposite corners, it was seen that they crossed at a point about two miles from Flag Spring, near the southern foot of Sugar Loaf Mountain.

That still left a lot of ground to be covered and the owner of the land was not much interested, since he had a sprawling ranch to take care of. Furthermore, he discouraged others from digging up his pastureland. In any event, no guarantee existed that the strange Roman numerals were connected to the buried gold.

There are quite a few points in José Lopat's yarn, given to his son, which fly in the face of history. Although I had

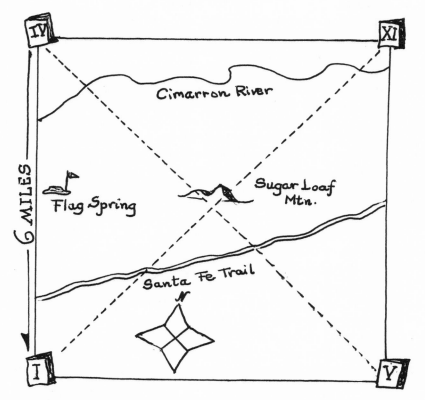

Map supposedly showing buried treasure near Flag Spring. Courtesy Marc Simmons Collection.

heard it repeated a number of times, I didn't put much stock in the whole account. Therefore, I was more than a little surprised by the telegram from my friend telling me that the legendary gold had been uncovered.

After a rash of excited stories in the country newspapers, it was finally revealed that the Hugoton fortune hunters had pulled off a neat hoax, merely for their own amusement. The bars of gold put on exhibit, which had caused townsfolk to grow goggle-eyed, were nothing but clumsy forgeries, little lead bricks coated with gilt. Someone remarked ruefully that the druggist, a ringleader in the affair, ought to change his name to P. T. Barnum.

While all the flurry was the result of a contrived circus, that means naturally that the secret of the Frenchmen's gold is yet kept safe at Flag Spring, or possibly at nearby Sugar Loaf Mountain. On the other hand, maybe the entire thing never really existed, but rather sprang from the fertile imagination of an old man named José Lopat.

27
Spanish Gold or Fraud?

The development of the mining industry in New Mexico awaited arrival of the railroad in 1880. With trains available at last to bring in heavy equipment and to carry out any ore that might be found, prospectors swarmed through the hills and mountains of the territory.

Unhappily, the railroads brought not only honest miners but also swindlers, called bunko men. They would salt a patch of ground with a little gold dust, then bring in a gullible investor. Usually an accomplice appeared, while buyer and seller were discussing terms, and bid up the claim. Many an innocent New Mexican got fleeced in this way. Greed seemed to override good sense. More innocent souls would have lost their shirts, except for vigilantes who kept the bunko men on the move and even stretched a neck or two when they didn't move fast enough.

Around the turn of the century, more sophisticated schemes were introduced and they became far larger in scope. One example, which eventually grabbed national headlines, had its start in Silver City in 1905. Local residents George DuBois and his son Lee announced that they had learned the location of a lost Spanish gold mine in the mountains near town. An old Indian had guided them to the site, they claimed.

The story was not entirely improbable. In the early 1800s, Spaniards from Chihuahua had mined copper at nearby Santa Rita, hauling it south in burro trains to Janos. Some of them could have found and quietly exploited a gold mine at the same time.

The DuBoises declared they needed capital to begin operations. Since money was scarce in Silver City, they went to Denver. There, they encountered a number of men eager to invest. One was a prominent dentist, Dr. R. C. Hunt. He at once put ten thousand dollars into the hat and was made president of the hastily incorporated Spanish Bullion Mining Company. Using the doctor's good name as a front, the DuBoises enlisted seven other leading Denverites as investors and directors.

Next, they placed large, eye-catching ads in New York and Boston newspapers, offering to sell stock. The prospects for profit were painted so enticingly that the money began to roll in, almost eighty thousand dollars in a few weeks. The company said it expected to obtain a million dollars through the sale. In Boston, Charles Riddiford, a young and ambitious federal investigator, saw one of the ads, thought its promises were too good to be true, and wrote for further information. When he showed the extravagant promotional brochures to his superior, he was

Workers at a mine entrance. Photograph by George C. Bennett; courtesy Museum of New Mexico.

given a green light to visit Silver City and take a firsthand look at the gold mine.

On the scene, Riddiford hired a couple of mining engineers, rented a buckboard, and drove up a canyon to the mine site. To him, it seemed little more than a large limestone cave with loose rock on the floor and no sign of valuable mineral. His engineers concurred. Immediately, he traveled to Denver and confronted the surprised father and son. They trotted out ore samples and assay reports as proof that gold did exist on their property. But after intense questioning, both men confessed to fraud.

Charges were quickly brought against all persons associated with the company. A U.S. attorney from Kansas City was imported to prosecute the case, and he told the press that this was one of "the rankest swindles ever perpetrated in the West." The trial proved a sensation and was closely followed by papers across the country. The DuBoises recanted their confession, swearing that it had been extracted under duress. And they hired an aggressive defense attorney.

The prosecution was able to parade a string of damaging witnesses. One of them was an old-time Silver City miner, Jack Flemming, who drawled that the Lord had created the limestone cave, but then forgotten to put any gold in to keep prospectors happy.

However, the defense was not without a star performer. He was a well-known mining engineer named Lindeman, who testified that he had visited the mine, observed evidence of Spanish excavations, and estimated the ore might be worth twenty million dollars.

The conflicting testimony must have confused the jury. The defendants tried to help their case by packing the audience with members of their families. The wives loudly wept and snuffled in their handkerchiefs throughout the proceedings. That added an air of melodrama. The jury deliberated for several hours before returning a guilty verdict. The Spanish Bullion Mine, in their judgment, was bogus. The judge handed George DuBois the stiffest sentence: thirty days in jail and a thousand-dollar fine. The others were assigned lesser penalties, with the lightest given to the dentist Hunt, who was considered a complete dupe. The judge lectured him sternly about being more careful with his investments.

It is said that this case attracted such public notice that Colorado and other western states were able to beef up their laws against wildcat speculation and fraudulent mining stock. In that regard at least, something good came out of the Dubois scheme. And then, of course, there were the true believers who ever after maintained that if the company had not been railroaded in court, it would have launched one of the richest mines in the entire West.

APPENDIX ONE

A WPA Tale Sampler

During the Great Depression of the 1930s, New Mexico was the beneficiary of several federally funded economic recovery programs. One of those under the Works Progress Administration (WPA) supported studies in history and folklore. Writers were offered jobs involving the collection of material from old-timers and others through personal interviews. One category gathered was the ever-popular lost-mine story. Four representative examples of the short WPA tales follow. The collected WPA original typescripts are preserved at Santa Fe, New Mexico, in the collections of the Palace of the Governors (Museum of New Mexico) and the State Records Center and Archives.

Treasure of the Plum

José Trujillo

The town of Las Placitas was settled in the late eighteenth century. It lay in the foothills of the Sandia Mountains, northeast of Albuquerque. The inhabitants were farmers and weekend treasure hunters. For years, they had told and retold among themselves the brief story of the *Tesoro de la Ciruela,* which is to say the Treasure of the Plum. Why it was called that has long since been forgotten.

The legend holds that when the Pueblo Indians rebelled in 1680, the Spanish survivors seized what valuables they could find and hid them. Some of their treasure they buried in the mountains east of Sandia Pueblo, not far from what later became the town of Ojo del Oso. Among the items they left were a bell and door from a mission church, two big bars of gold, and many bars of silver.

In their years of hunting, the Las Placitas people dug up an entire mountainside. But their efforts led to no results. Their descendants say that the Sandia Indians know the treasure's location and continue to keep a guard over it to this very day.

The Padre's Mine at Cañon de la Soledad

Cleofas M. Jaramillo

On the trail at El Paso del Norte was a Spanish mission under the charge of Father La Rue. He not only converted

146

the Indians, but also gave shelter to weary travelers going north or south, when that region belonged to Spain.

One night, just as the padre was closing the mission gates, a lone traveler entered and collapsed at his feet. Seeing that it was a Spanish soldier, the padre, with the assistance of his servant, took the stranger into the mission. While dressing his wounds, the priest noticed a long string of gold nuggets hanging about the man's neck.

For two days, the good priest took care of the stranger. On the third night, realizing that his end was near, the soldier called Padre La Rue and gave him the gold nuggets, saying that they came from a great pocket of nuggets that he had discovered in a lonely canyon near El Paso, but that he had been attacked by a band of Indians and forced to flee before he could secure all the gold.

After describing the location of the canyon and instructing the priest to go north a certain distance from the mouth of the canyon to a big rock marked with the drawing of an Indian head, the stranger died.

The padre left the mission and went in quest of the gold pocket. With the accurate description, Father La Rue did not have much difficulty in finding the Cañon de la Soledad and the gold located inside a cave under a great bluff. Upon removing the nuggets from a pocket, he discovered a rich vein which lay underneath. He sealed the mouth of the cave and took the nuggets to the mission, where he buried them in a corner of the courtyard. From time to time, he went back and worked the gold vein.

The news of the great wealth that the priest had accumulated reached the bishop of Durango and he sent men for the priest. Someone informed La Rue that they were coming after him, and he abandoned the mission, taking with him his gold treasure. He sought shelter in an Indian pueblo of his parish, but the Indians proved treacherous. They robbed the padre and murdered him.

Afterward, the ruins of a log cabin, in which Padre La Rue had lived while working the mine, and a forge, in which he melted his gold, were found. Treasure hunters have since searched Soledad Canyon for the fabulous gold mine, but the cave has never been found.

Buried Money on the Mimbres River

FRANCES E. TOTTY

Pedro Raesequeon came to Grant County, New Mexico, in 1880 from Mexico and settled on the Mimbres River, near the present site of the Mimbres post office. Mr. Raesequeon was a freighter by trade and always freighted into Grant County to the various points of importance from the lower Rio Grande Valley and Mexico.

Mr. Raesequeon, when he came to the Mimbres, was about thirty years old. He and his wife started a small ranch, which she took care of while he was away from home freighting. The family often stayed at home entirely, and when it became necessary to buy any groceries at the store, they never purchased them, but traded eggs, butter, and other products for their meager supplies. If the family ever spent any money no one ever knew about it, unless Mr. Raesequeon spent some money on his trips to Mexico and the lower Rio Grande.

They had the barest necessities of life, but it was a known fact that they were making money from the freighter line as well as on the small ranch they owned, for they were a group of thrifty people. Mr. Raesequ⟨   ⟩., in 1918, sold a part of his ranch for seventeen thousand dollars in cash, but was not known to place the money in a bank, and his son, Manuel Raesequeon of Mimbres, New Mexico, says that he is positive his father buried the money along with all that he had acquired during his long period of freighting to Grant County's various small towns of the early days.

A small part of the money was found at one time in 1935, it is believed. But it might have been money that was buried by someone else. It was found by Manuel. The family still have ranch holdings in Mexico. Pedro Raesequeon died in 1935, at the age of eighty-five. Some of his buried money may someday be recovered, but it is doubtful.

Just across the road from the Raesequeon house is the old Ancheta place, where Louis Ancheta moved when he left Pinos Altos to settle on the Mimbres. Ancheta came to Pinos Altos around 1860, after escaping from Old Mexico, having taken part in a revolution. Louis fatally wounded his father, who before his death placed a curse on his son, Louis Ancheta—the curse being that Louis would marry and have a large family and that every child would disgrace the Ancheta name, and that Louis would acquire a large fortune and would not ever enjoy the pleasures that money would give.

When Louis Ancheta settled at Pinos Altos, only a few people were there. But afterward the place was flooded with miners and prospectors, all in search of gold. Louis Ancheta soon found that he could acquire a fortune by buying the virgin gold.

Louis Ancheta married the daughter of a rancher near Pinos Altos, and a short time after their marriage they decided to move to the Mimbres River, near the present site of the Mimbres post office.

The gold was moved from the Ancheta home in Pinos Altos to the Mimbres in large [wooden] champagne boxes that were held together with screws. Robert Stevens, a youngster living at the time in Pinos Altos, said that all of the boxes were sealed but one, and that it was only partly filled. After he was grown and knew the value of gold and weights, Stevens estimated that there was probably 150,000 dollars worth of bullion stored in those boxes.

The Ancheta family all seemed to be under the curse of their grandfather and came to some tragic end. Juan Ancheta of San Lorenzo, grandson of Louis Ancheta, will allow anyone to dig for the bullion, which his grandfather buried [and never recovered]. But he isn't interested in searching for the gold himself.

Treasure

RAMITOS MONTOYA

Time and again, I have heard stories about hidden treasures in New Mexico. The following tale was told to me by my old uncle.

Some Spanish people had a treasure, which they piled in bags in an old wagon and made their way toward the mountains at Fort Union. The heavy load was pulled by mules. The men were ambushed, killed, and the gold stolen.

The five robbers agreed to hide the treasure and take only part of the gold at a time. The treasure was buried together with the bodies of the murdered men. In order to relocate the exact spot, the bandits inscribed some words on a rock: "Dig three feet to the right. Keep on digging."

As time passed, four of the men died. The remaining member of the band wrote a note about the treasure, a note found much later by his son. It read as follows:

There is a hidden treasure on top of the big pine mountain. Dig three feet to the right. At first you will find some human bones but do not be alarmed. I possess part of this treasure. The others that had part were Juan Rubio, Carlos Nuño, José Aldano, and Juan Luna. Please tell the sons of my above friends about this treasure.

> Your father,
> B. Pérez

The Pérez boys, together with the sons of the other men, went to look for the treasure. To keep their courage up, they drank whiskey to their heart's content. They worked all day but did not accomplish much, for they were under the influence of liquor. They soon fell asleep. Then, others who were watching what the lads were doing, came and carried the treasure away.

Treasure Items from the Newspapers

A Note on the Adams Diggings

From *Silver City Enterprise*, December 7, 1888:

Silver City, NM—The papers of the territory are in error in stating that Adams of "Adams diggins" fame is dead. He is now living in Encinada [*sic*], near San Diego. He has already spent three fortunes seeking for the lost diggins, and hopes to be able to find them yet or spend another fortune in the attempt.

A Hint to Prospectors

From *Silver City Enterprise*, September 4, 1891:

The *Enterprise* desires to call the attention of prospectors to the fact that they have for many years been passing over valuable deposits of marble, onyx and jasper, which in all probability are of as great and possibly of more permanent value than any gold or silver mine in the world. Take for instance the marble quarries of Carrera, Italy which have been in operation for hundreds of years and will continue to be worked for centuries to come. We have within the limits of Grant County, New Mexico, a greater variety of the grades of marble than found in the same area anywhere on earth. Note the different kinds enumerated below.

The serpentine rock with the newly manufactured name of Ricolite found on the Gila River near Carlisle is a beautiful ornamental stone for architectural ornaments. It is banded with alternate strata of gray and green colors from one half to one inch in thickness. It rapidly gained the front rank in favor in the east, and the demand is greater than the supply, for the reason that transportation facilities are meagre. It is susceptible of a fine finish and is quite durable. This is probably the only deposit of it in the world, as no mention is made of such a rock in any work on geology or lithology.

The marbles of Bear Creek, ten miles from Silver City, will without doubt attract a great deal of attention in the near future. The black marble is of a jet black color, the variegated marbles of the same series are as fine as can be found anywhere, very even in texture and susceptible of a very high polish. Within the next year these quarries will be shipping large quantities east and west as there is a great demand for the kind of marble found there.

The white sculptural marble of the Hanover district is said to be equal to Italian marble for sculptors' use; the quarry has not been opened sufficiently to show its full merit but from surface indications the deposit is extensive, and when a little depth below the influence of the waving elements on the surface is reached, the few flaws found on top will no doubt disappear. Add to the above jasper of the finest quality found in the Tres Hermanas range below Deming, and as we are informed never yet located or developed. A few weeks ago a gentleman exhibited in this office a pair of sleeve buttons and a ring cut from this valuable and beautiful stone which he said he found on a vein in the Tres Hermanas seveal years ago. The samples shown equal anything of the kind to be found in Egypt.

Then again gold stone is known to exist in large deposits in the mountain range northeast of Hudson's Hot Springs, between Hudson's and the Mimbres. While prospecting for the precious metals look out for valuable architectural, ornamental and jewel stones. Many of these rocks when broken show but little sign of their true value but when placed upon a grind stone and smoothed or polished, their beauties begin to appear. When you are in doubt take your samples to where you can test them in this way, and you may find yourself the possessor of a fortune you little dreamed of.

A Bizarre Hoax

From *Santa Fe New Mexican*, March 7, 1896:

STORY OF HIDDEN TREASURE

A BRAZILIAN COLONEL ENGAGED IN THE TASK OF
EXPLORING LA GRAN QUIVIRA

PROFESSES TO HAVE FOUND VAST RICHES

VERBATIM REPORT OF AN INTERVIEW WITH THE STRANGE
MAN—WHAT HE HAS FOUND. AMOUNT OF BURIED
COIN—ABOUT HIS PLANS

The other day there arrived in this city of Santa Fe an interesting personage. He bears a passport from the Brazilian consul in Peru, in which "the bearer" is described as being a Colonel in the Brazilian Army, 23 years of age, single, and his name is given as Juan Miguel de la Cerda.

As soon as it was known that the Colonel was in the city, a representative of the *New Mexican*, accompanied by Major George H. Pratt of Laguna, called to see him. Appended is a verbatim report of the conversation that ensued.

INITIAL QUERY AND ANSWER

Reporter—Colonel, I am a representative of our newspaper, the *New Mexican*, and have called on you for the purpose of getting some information concerning your excavations in the ruins of Chilili and La Gran Quivira. Are you willing to tell me, for the information of the public, who you are, what progress you have made, and what caused you to come to the particular part of this country that you have selected.

In reply the affable young Colonel said: *Je suis charme de vous voir*. I am always delighted to see and converse with representatives of the press. They are the most enterprising people I have met in this great country. Their gracious cordiality is a wonderful thing. Certainly, sir, it will afford me pleasure to give you all the information you ask. It is not fate alone that brought me to this country. I am a native of Brazil and a Colonel in the regular army of that country. My father is a Brazilian and my mother is a native of Spain. She comes from the illustrious family of La Cerda. I am quite a linguist, being able to speak fluently eleven languages and to write seven of them. While pursuing my studies in Spain, I became very much interested in the

155

ancient archives of that Country. In my researches I found the original reports sent to Spain from the then province of New Mexico, and became very much interested in the information they contained. I have copies in my possession and maps that have guided me to the place I have selected for excavation.

VALUABLE ANTIQUITIES DISCOVERED

Reporter—Have you discovered anything of value yet?

Colonel—My first work was at Chilili. You have already seen in the Albuquerque papers a list of the valuable collections of Antiquities that I found at that place. The collection, which is equivalent to a treasure, I will present to the Historical Society of New Mexico with my compliments. My great work, however, will be at Gran Quivira where my camp is established at present. I have already done considerable work there with very gratifying results.

Reporter—Have you found anything at the Gran Quivira?

Colonel—Yes, indeed. As a matter of fact, I already knew what was there and where it was. La Gran Quivira was the most flourishing Spanish settlement in this country as far back as 370 years ago. The people were mostly gold and copper miners. A whole block was occupied by goldsmiths and the work of their hands was the most wonderful and exquisite in the world.

There is at this time a crown of filigree gold set with emeralds and turquoise in possession of the royal family of Spain. This was made in Gran Quivira and is a marvel of beauty and workmanship. During the first week of my work there, I found a cavern where $60,000,000 in gold are buried. At another place I found a large number of beautiful marble statues, brought to this country from Spain

and Rome. The most artistic thing I have found is a golden
.sacred heart belonging to the ancient cathedral. All these
treasures I have left buried for a while, just where they
were, until I can secure protection from the government.
You can readily see that it would not be safe for me to
uncover that sum of money unless I had some protection.*

Reporter—In what shape is the gold you found? Bars?

Colonel—All the gold is in coin stamped with the busts
of Charles I, Charles II, Charles III, and Charles IV.

Reporter—What do you propose to do with so much
money?

Colonel—I am going to bring a colony of a thousand
families from Brazil to cultivate coffee in the lovely valley.

At this point, Major Pradt remarked that he was at Gran
Quivira last Christmas, and that the thermometer was 15
degrees below zero, and that such a cold country might
not be suitable for the cultivation of coffee.

The Colonel promptly replied by saying: You never can
tell what you can do until you try. Nature is a wonderful
thing. I am sure that coffee trees will become acclimated
in the course of time.

Editor's Note. The reader will easily recognize that these paragraphs
contain nothing but the preposterous fabrications of the "Colonel."

A GRAND CATHEDRAL CONTEMPLATED

The Colonel, continuing the conversation, said: I am
to build a grand cathedral, but the ancient one I am
going to leave intact as a monument to me, the discov-
erer of the treasures that so many have sought in vain. I
will use the material from the main ruins of the build-

ings for houses for my people. I am going to employ a very celebrated architect from Washington by the name of Neeli to come and superintend the work of my cathedral and other buildings.

I am now preparing the plans, and those of the cathedral I will submit to his grace, the archbishop, for his approval.

Reporter—I understand that the country around Gran Quivira is devoid of water and not suitable for farming.

Colonel—It was true at one time, but not so now. I discovered a spring of water with such force that it threw big boulders forty feet in the air. Near the source of this spring, I am going to erect a monument in honor of the Franciscan missionaries who did so much faithful work for Christianity.

Reporter—It has been said that you are going to marry a young girl of the village of Tajique. Is it true?

The Colonel, with sparkling eyes, raised his gaze to heaven: "I thank the God of my fathers that it is true. In a couple of months, my family will arrive from Europe to witness my marriage to one of the most lovely, most accomplished, and most modest [young ladies] in the world. I will devote my whole life to make her the happiest of mortals. I will make her the owner of my treasures and the sweetest companion of my fame and renown."

Reporter—Is everything you have just told me, true?

Colonel—*La mentira es la verguenza del hombre.* The lie is the shame of man. What I have told you is absolutely true.

Thus ended the interview with this remarkable man, who has created almost as much excitement in some quarters in one month as the meek Francis Schlatter [New Mexico's religious healer] did in a year.

From *Santa Fe New Mexican*, March 11, 1896:

MR. DOW'S PLAIN DENIAL

HE SAYS THAT
COLONEL JUAN MIGUEL DE LA CERDA
IS POSITIVELY NOT GOING TO MARRY HIS DAUGHTER

To the Editor of the New Mexican:

Tajique, N.M. March 8—I see that some of the New Mexican papers are reporting that a man calling himself Colonel Juan Miguel de la Cerda is to marry one of my daughters.

This statement is false. The so-called Colonel has been at my place a few times and even came after being told to keep away. Finally, on last Friday morning I had to publicly run him away and warn him not to come any more.

I have no doubt that he is a Gypsy fraud by the company he keeps. A person can't think otherwise.

E. A. Dow

From *Santa Fe New Mexican*, April 3, 1896:
Merchant E. A. Dow of Tajique writes that he has been receiving threatening letters from Colonel Juan Miguel de la Cerda, the Brazilian adventurer, who is now in Trinidad, Colorado. Mr. Dow declares him a fraud and he declares that the public should be warned against him.

POSTSCRIPT

Col. Ralph E. Twitchell in his *Leading Facts of New Mexican History*, published in 1912, includes the following note on this curious affair:

It was at Chilili that one hears for the first time the stories of buried treasures and treasure hunting expeditions. Less than two decades ago, so the visitor is seriously informed, a Brazilian succeeded in lifting the hidden gold underneath the altar of the old church. For weeks he had employed men digging within the ruins of the sanctuary. Then came the hour when he announced that the next day he would unearth the treasure and would divided it with the people.

During the night, however, his men made away with it. The people of Chilili sought to wreck vengeance on the Brazilian, who remained, but the proposed lynching was averted.

Lost Spanish Mine Found

From *Santa Fe New Mexican*, September 28, 1969:

Lincoln, N.M. (AP)—A Lincoln prospector who devoted 19 years to the search claims he has found a lost 18th century Spanish silver and gold mine on the east slope of the Capitan Mountains in central New Mexico.

Herman Philpot, owner of the J & J Mining Co. of Lincoln, says he discovered the lost mine after using an old map and then noticing silver nuggets that had washed out of a spring. He began excavations near the spring and found an old tunnel hidden by a cave-in.

Philpot said the tunnel runs 500 yards back into the mountainside in Box Canyon.

"The (ore) veins where I've dug are as much as 12 feet wide and they're awful good in hair silver, uranium, platinum, copper, asbestos, gold, silver with some manganese and hematite ore in the same mine," Philpot said.

Philpot has owned claims to lost mines in the area since 1950. He says he has been a prospector for 40 years.

The prospector said the mine is believed to have been operated about 1784. It is known locally as the Old Lost Spanish Cave.

He said he found evidence of a crude smelter in the area where silver was refined. He also found a rusted Spanish spur, shell cases from the late 1700s [?], and bones he believes to be those of the early miners.

The prospector theorizes the miners may have been killed or driven off by unfriendly Indians in the area.

He said he might try to sell the mining rights to his find. Philpot made no estimate of the mine's worth.

Selected References

Bancroft, Caroline. "Lost-Mine Legends of Colorado." *California Folklore Quarterly*, vol. 2 (October 1943), pp. 253–63.

Busher, Jimmie. *Lost Mines and Treasures of the Southwest.* Mesilla Park, N.M.: Treasure Guide Publication Company, 1975.

Carson, Kit. "That $100,000 Loot in the Malpais Country." *True West* (July–August 1962), pp. 24–26.

Dobie, J. Frank. *Apache Gold and Yaqui Silver.* Boston: Little Brown, 1939.

―――. *Coronado's Children.* New York: Grosset and Dunlap, 1930.

Douglas, Jack. *Gold in Lost Mines.* Lodi, Calif.: The Old Prospector, 1951.

Eberhart, Perry. *Treasure Tales of the Rockies.* New York: Ballantine Books, 1973.

162

Granger, Byrd Howell. *A Motif Index for Lost Mines and Treasures Applied to Redaction of Arizona Legends.* Tucson: University of Arizona Press, 1977.

Jameson, W. C. *Buried Treasure of the American Southwest.* Little Rock: August House, 1989.

Kay, Eleanor. "Lost Mines and Buried Gold." *New Mexico Magazine,* vol. 12 (September 1935), pp. 20–21; 44–45.

Koury, Phil A. "Treasure of Victorio Peak." *American West,* vol. 24 (October 1987), pp. 58–65.

Lottritz, J. Martin. "Lure of Lost Mines." *New Mexico Magazine,* vol. 14 (October 1937), pp. 12–13; 38–39.

McKenna, James A. *Black Range Tales.* Reprint ed. Glorieta, N.M.: Rio Grande Press, 1969.

Mitchell, John D. *Lost Mines and Buried Treasures along the Old Frontier.* Palm Desert, Calif.: Desert Magazine Press, 1953.

———. *Lost Mines of the Great Southwest.* Phoenix: Press of the Journal, 1933.

Penfield, Thomas. *Dig Here!* San Antonio: The Naylor Company, 1962.

———. *A Guide to Treasure in New Mexico.* Deming, N.M.: Carson Enterprises, 1981.

Probert, Thomas. *Lost Mines and Buried Treasure of the West—Bibliography and Place Names.* Berkeley: University of California Press, 1977.

Smith, C. C. "More about the Lost Adams Gold Diggings." *Frontier Times,* vol. 5 (April 1928), pp. 318–19.

Tenny, A. M., Jr. "The Lost Adams Gold Diggings." *Frontier Times,* vol. 5 (March 1928), pp. 240–48.

Willison, George. *Here They Dug the Gold.* New York: A. L. Burt Company, 1931.